MENDING BOOKS IS FUN

by

BROOKE BYRNE
Staff, Lynn Public Library
Lynn, Massachusetts

BURGESS PUBLISHING COMPANY
426 South Sixth Street — Minneapolis 15, Minn.

L.O.
Z271
B95

Copyright 1956
by
Brooke Byrne

2nd Printing 1957

"It's Never too Late to Mend"

Printed in the United States of America

PREFACE

IN WHICH I TRY TO EXPLAIN THAT I'M NOT REALLY NUTS, Or, If I Am, I'm in Awfully Good Company.

My publisher says that nobody reads prefaces.

So you, if you are reading this, are the exception, and we can practically chat in private. Drag up a chair while I explain how this book came to be.

Back in the thirties I went into library work, and got mending. In those days, the idea that mending books could be fun would have startled me into a fit. That was the era of the paper hinge and the starch-based paste--the stuff that went rancid in summer, remember? Yet even before that was the era of the pot of mucilage melting on a Sterno. It's small wonder that mending has always been the bottom of the barrel in library work. It was pure built-in frustration, because in plain fact you <u>couldn't</u> mend a book. All you could do was stave off disintegration for a little while. Year after year, books that could never be replaced slipped out of your hands into the incinerator. If you had a feeling for books--and why else would you be working in a library?--it was heartbreaking. Book-mending <u>fun</u>? It was not. It was the salt-mines.

During the late unpleasantness overseas I went into another line of work, and only came back to the library a

-i-few years ago. It took me a little while to realize that things had happened in the mending field. The market was alive with new products and gadgets, all promising. I was extraordinarily lucky in having a Chief who values books for their own sake; the minute I told her that it seemed possible now to really mend a book she gave me carte blanche to try anything and everything.

Which I did.

And the result is here. I found that other librarians across the country had made the same happy discovery; we've swapped ideas and compared techniques, until, now, it seems possible that we have enough tested know-how to justify this book.

But here's where you come in. I know for sure that this is not the last word on mending. It's just a sort of progress-report to the profession, presented in the hope that lots of menders will be encouraged to experiment and develop even simpler and better ways of preserving our collections. The publisher says that if this goes well and there seems to be any interest, we can have a second edition--in which anything you contribute will be incorporated. (By the way, do you like the blue ink? It's a departure from orthodox printing, but I like it--and everything in the book is unorthodox. It sort of seems to fit.)

So if anyone anywhere wants to pitch in with a suggestion, or even an argument, you'll be welcome. Come on in, the water's fine. Anybody can get into the act. Book-repair is an expanding, developing field in library work and we need to get together on it.

I'd like to thank--among a great many others--for their encouragment, help and suggestions: Miss Gene Kubal, School Librarian, Crown Point, Indiana; Miss Ruth Carmean, School Librarian, Santa Cruz High School, California; Mrs. George (V. Genevieve) Galick, Director, Division of Library Extension of the Massachusetts Department of Education; Hardin Craig, Jr., Librarian, Rice Institute, Houston, Texas; Miss Elizabeth Thalman, Librarian, Hobart and William Smith College, Geneva, New York; Mrs. Henry (Louise) Boudreau, Chairman of Public Relations, Massachusetts Library Association; Mrs. Ruth S. Wikoff, Librarian, General Library, University of Texas, Houston, Texas; Miss Gertrude R. Metcalf, School Librarian, Bellwood-Antis Public Schools, Bellwood, Pennsylvania. And very especially Miss Thelma R. King and her staff of the Steele Memorial Library of Chemung County, Elmira, New York.

And to all the librarians, but extra-specially the menders, of the North Shore Library Association (and Mrs. Charles Haywood who invited me) and of the Merrimac Valley Library Association, my thanks for patiently listening to me sound off and responding with all manner of good ideas.

You see how much I owe to other people; it couldn't have been done alone. And I haven't begun to list all the people who have helped--some of them just by a casual remark at a convention, or a paragraph in a professional publication.

But since we're alone here in the preface, I might as well admit that this book would never have happened at all if it weren't for the fact that the Lynn Public Library has a Chief Librarian, Miss Louise B. Day, who has had all kinds of professional distinction but--as I can testify-- is most specially remarkable for her love of books. She has instituted an Audio-Visual Room, and we have, thanks to her, a microfilming gadget, but her first love is books; and all I can wish to menders everywhere is that they should have a Chief like Miss Day.

Finally, I'd better admit my debt to the pages, past and present, at the Lynn Public Library. They do our mending, and they have brow-beaten, badgered and bedevilled me into finding the answers to hard questions contained in this book.

So now let's get on with it. Mending, anyone?

Lynn, Massachusetts

January, 1956

CONTENTS

	Page
PREFACE	i

CHAPTER
1 - THE CORPUS DELICTI, or --
   What's It All About? 1
2 - DON'T SHOOT THE BINDER, or --
   Well, Don't! 9
3 - PASS THE AMMUNITION, or --
   Where, What and How Much? 11
4 - A NECESSARY PARENTHESIS WHICH
   YOU REALLY SHOULDN'T SKIP 25
5 - TIME AND MOTION, or --
   We, Too, Can Be Efficiency
   Engineers 29
6 - EASY DOES IT, or --
   Two For the Money 33
7 - SMALL FRY, or --
   Odds and Ends for Spare Moments 43
8 - OPERATING THEATER, or --
   The Expert to the Rescue 49
9 - BACKING UP, or --
   Why, When and How to Replace a Spine 59
10 - MASTERPIECES, or --
   Re-Casing, Which the Experts Say
   Can't be Done 67
11 - PREVENTIVE MEDICINE, or --
   An Apple for the Teacher-Librarian 75
12 - THE LOWER DEPTHS, or --
   Juvenile Delinquents 81
13 - MIRACLE IN THE STACKS, or --
   In Re: Reference Departments 89
14 - BEAUTY SALON, or --
   There's Nothing Like Leather 95
15 - FANCY TOUCHES, or --
   Anybody Can Do Anything 103

16 - THE MYSTIQUE, or --
         Why Are Menders? 121
17 - DO-IT-YOURSELF, or --
         Why EVERYBODY Needs This Book 129

GLOSSARY 141

INDEX 151

Chapter One
THE CORPUS DELICTI
or
What's It All About?

The first step in learning to repair a book is to take a book and tear it apart.

Obviously, if you're going to reconstruct a book, you'd better know how it was put together in the first place. The easiest way to find out is to take a book and look at it, inside and out. Pick, for choice, a novel printed within the past ten years (war-time books are special, and pretty horrible.)

We have, to begin with, the outside of the book. This is generally spoken of as the "binding" but the proper technical term is "casing" (there is a considerable difference between a bound book and a cased one.) The "casing" consists of two stiff side-covers and a cloth spine, or back (Fig. 1). The side-covers are made of heavy cardboard. Over them is glued some sort of cloth or paper covering, frequently the kind of dyed stuff you'd rather not be caught carrying in the rain. This cloth or paper extends from one edge of the front cover to the far edge of the back cover, being folded over and glued inside the cover edges.

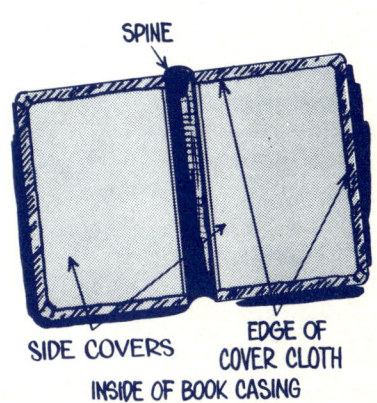

Figure 1

Between the covers is a space slightly larger than the bulk of the contents; this

-1-

stretch of plain cloth is usually reinforced with heavy paper and forms the "spine" or back of the book. (Fig.2). This is where the title, author's name, publisher's imprint, and so on appear.

Figure 2

That is the "casing" of a modern book.

The inside of the book is the "contents." This is the printed material. Look at your book.

You observe that the pages are clumped together in sections, ordinarily eight folded sheets laid one inside the other and stitched with rather fragile thread. (Fig. 3). These groups of pages are known as "signatures," and the rather interesting reason for this will be found in the glossary, if you care. Right now, all you need to notice is that these signatures are not put together in a flat pile. Rather, they are shaped into a curve-- convex at the spine, concave at the edge of the pages. It's not a very noticeable curve but it's there and it's important. A square-cut book--they are made--doesn't last very long.

Now, with a grin of fiendish glee, rip your book apart. (ASIDE TO CHIEF LIBRARIANS: It's all right, we'll put it back together again as good as new. That's the whole purpose of this

Figure 3

What's It All About?   3

treatise.)

What do we find? We find that across the backs of the signatures there's a strip of coarse cheesecloth (technically known as "super") glued solidly onto the signatures and extending about an inch on either side. (Fig.4).

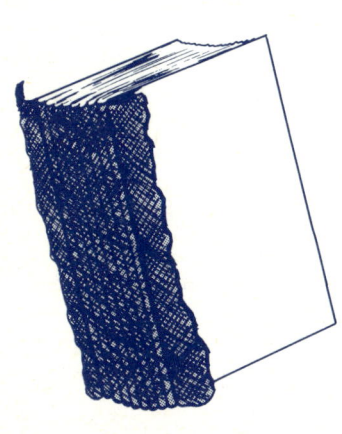

This "super" has hidden itself neatly under the end-papers (these haven't been mentioned up to now, but they are about to get a whole paragraph to themselves. Don't rush me.) In fact, this strip of cheesecloth makes the hinges which hold the "casing" and the "contents" together.

Now you see the reason for end-papers. They are not properly a part of the contents, nor yet of the casing. They're at once a disguise and a reinforcement. They are sheets of heavy paper--heavier at

Figure 4

least than the stock upon which the contents is printed. Often they bear maps, or handsome art work, or elaborate tables connected with the subject of the book. Artists make a nice thing out of creating end-papers for the more solvent publishers. But plain or fancy, their function is two-fold. Let's observe what it is.

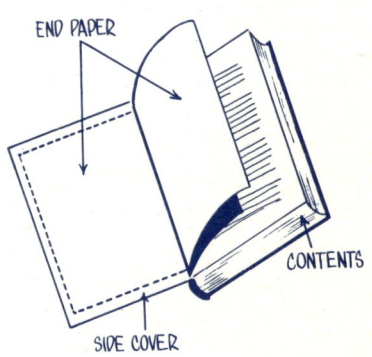

Figure 5

Open your book at the front. Observe that the front end-paper is a single sheet the size of the opened book. (Fig.5). One half is glued down solidly over the inside of the cover, hiding the edges of the cover-cloth, and the strip of "super" as well. But now we must look very closely indeed to note something very important.

At the hinge--at the point where the casing is attached to the contents--the contents flares out in a sort of lip or rim or flange, created by the rondure of the signatures which we noted previously. (Fig. 6). This lip or rim is known to book-makers as "the ledge" and the idea of creating it is a milestone in the history of bookmaking. If it weren't there, your book would never survive handling at all. And now you observe that the end-paper is fastened down, with a light touch of paste, <u>over</u> the ledge and thus attached to the actual contents for about a quarter of an inch. The rest of the sheet flaps free to form the first page of the book.

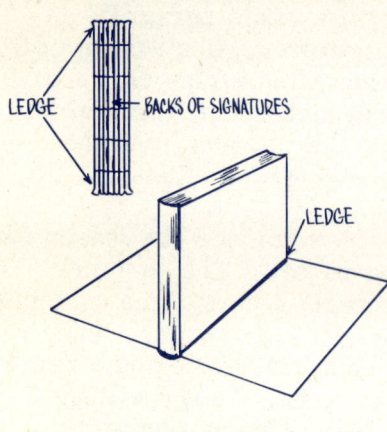

Figure 6

Often a quite extraneous page is attached to the inside of this free end-paper--forming a false title page in front, or just a blank page at the end of the book. There is probably a reason for this, though on the face of it it looks like pure defiance of the pulp-wood shortage. All we care is to note that it is sometimes so.

You see, this juncture-point between casing and contents is the place where books start to disintegrate, and therefore we have to understand exactly how it is made. And in so studying it, we discover at once that it isn't very sturdy. Quite often a brisk twitch of an end-paper will detach it immediately from the ledge and the contents. A butter-fingered borrower (are there any other kinds?) will test its strength even on the very first circulation.

What's It All About?

And if all this sounds complex--well, you've got a book there, haven't you? Learn by doing--or rather, by un-doing. The publisher has promised all manner of useful illustrations to help out, but what you really need is a book to pull apart.

So now you have an eviscerated book in front of you, and you can see that what really holds the book together is the glue.

Brown, isn't it?

And if the book you've chosen as a sacrifice to science is more than a year old--isn't the glue <u>hard</u>! Cracks off at a touch.

Animal glue, likely.

And there, precisely, is the trouble.

Obviously what is needed is a glue that is flexible, elastic, non-cracking--one that won't dry out even in un-air-conditioned stacks or when left on top of radiators by our borrowers.

It exists.

Science, probably in the course of looking for something else, has produced precisely this miracle, and it's on the market under a whole galaxy of trade names. It's more expensive than old-fashioned glue, paste, and so on. BUT it makes possible book-repair which really does repair, and for keeps, books which would otherwise have to be discarded or re-bound. It's known technically as polyvinyl acetate, but we'll call it "plastic adhesive", which seems a reasonable description. It's creamy-white, water-soluble, tricky as a monkey until you learn how to use it, and pure magic for mending books (and just about everything else in the world, except maybe bathing caps.)

Its great virtue is that it stays flexible. This is also its one drawback.

The thing is, this stuff continues to absorb water from the atmosphere, whereas most other forms of paste or glue dry out and stay dry unless literally soaked. Comes a hot spell, the plastic adhesive gets dry--but on the first damp day, it reabsorbs a bit of moisture from the air and is as good as new again. This goes on and on, and the results are fine unless you are mending books in the Sahara, and Carnegie put very few of his libraries there.

Drawback: too much moisture, such as may arise from the book being deposited in a mud-puddle or read

while the borrower is taking a bath, makes the stuff as tacky as if it had never dried at all, and this can be embarrassing, since it will then stick to anything with which it comes in contact-- and naturally, if you have used it to put in a hinge, what it comes in contact with is the opposite side of the hinge.

What's It All About?

There is a very simple solution for this (though it took us a surprising while to think of it.) All you need do is waterproof the surface of a hinge or any other surface--such as the backs of the signatures--which have been treated with plastic adhesive. The least expensive wax for the job is ordinary household wax--paraffin--the stuff you melt down to cover jams and jellies. It is colorless, cheap, and works beautifully. Its use obviates the one objection to plastic adhesive.

This treatise, then, will deal with modern mending techniques based on the use of plastic adhesive. These techniques will _not_ work with old-fashioned glue, paste, or applied stickum. The simplicity, ease and effectiveness of these new techniques are going to sound like pipe-dreams to menders brought up--as I was--on the paper hinge. All I can say is--try 'em. They work.

Chapter Two
DON'T SHOOT THE BINDER
or
Well, Don't!

Some books must be re-bound.

Your basic collection must go to the bindery, budget or no; and it is wise to consider that the repair-techniques advocated here will often make it impossible for a binder to work on a book. His screams will be heard for miles. It's up to the librarian in charge of mending to decide whether a given book is of lasting value, and therefore ought to be re-bound promptly, or whether it should be mended and preserved for circulation over a period of years-- say ten--and then discarded.

The choice isn't really difficult. Books of lasting value are scarce enough nowadays so that it won't break you to bind the rare few.

And on the other side of the ledger--you do not have to re-bind all the copies of a best-seller. Give the bindery one, for the record; the rest can be mended and circulated until the furore dies down. Light love stories, mysteries, westerns, and the general froth of publishing can be kept moving as long as there is any demand for them, and then discarded with a clear conscience. This keeps the stacks from bulging.

Better still, it is now possible to repair a book which

has already been re-bound, or even a book which time has so dried out that the paper is too brittle for the bindery's operations. It is, as we shall see, possible to repair any and every book in any collection if you feel so inclined.

You see, the whole approach to binding and mending has to be revised--and the result is a fine, large saving on the budget. As I started out by saying, it's a revolution.

It's also fun.

NOTE: Be kind to salesmen. You never know when an absent-minded genius in a green eye-shade will come up with another miracle. Very few salesmen, unfortunately, have ever actually mended a book, but once in a while along comes a rare bird who really has something. He's worth cultivating.

Chapter Three
PASS THE AMMUNITION
or
Where, What and How Much?

We start with an obvious remark.

Only the plush and plutocratic libraries have Mending Departments. What everybody else has is a corner of a work-table and some floor or shelf space to pile up waiting books. Maybe the luxury of a book-truck for the finished product, while it waits to be revised. And a small portion of the general supply closet for mending materials.

Ain't it the truth, brethren?

Mind you, if you can con the Front Office into providing a whole table, or even a converted coat-closet all for your own, hop to it and more power to you. But the late lamented Mr. Carnegie apparently took a dim view of book-repair, or maybe never heard of it--come to think of it, he didn't supply any new books with his libraries, so he likely never gave a thought to tired old ones--and mostly menders have to cram in where they can.

Well, it's no use crying. We can manage.

What do you need, nowadays, to repair books?

What follows is a complete list of materials, valid until somebody thinks up something new--which might be tomorrow. This list is rock-bottom basic; you'll need everything on it. (Don't wince; it's surprisingly inexpensive, honest.) I'd suggest, though, that if you can possibly afford it, and have a large collection to care for, you invest in, first, a paper-cutter and second, a book-press. You can get along fine without them, to be sure, but they speed things up and add a lot of efficiency.

First of all, there are the things which you probably have on hand, even if you have to swipe them from your colleagues (and, of course, periodically swipe them back again.) Naturally it would be nice to have them all to yourself, and I urge that you campaign to that end, but even if you have them all labelled and shut away, you and I know that they'll be "borrowed" anyway.

- scissors
- ruler (perferably a fifteen-incher with a steel ferule)
- a plain pencil and a red pencil
- an eraser and an art-gum
- old newspapers

Now for what you'll have to beg, borrow, steal or even purchase out of petty cash:

- one (or better still, two) paring knives
- industrial waste-cloth
- an assortment of empty jars
- a wire suede-brush
- a box of kitchen waxed paper (not a roll; the kind that comes in sheets)
- household wax
- heavy wrapping paper

All of these items require explanation, and this is now coming up.

The knife is just a good, honest paring knife. I suggest two, so that one can have a sharp point and one a fairly

Where, What and How Much?

blunt tip. If you must choose, select the blunt-pointed type; if you have on hand a sharp-pointed knife, blunt the point. (This can be done on a knife-sharpener, if you have one, or you can ask the help of your janitor. Custodians are marvellously useful to menders. They think we're peculiar, but they rally round with a nice mixture of kindliness and curiosity.) If you are wondering why a blunt point, and I suppose you are, I explain that when you are skinning the cover-cloth off a book, as you will presently be doing, a sharp-pointed knife is very apt to skive through the dry and weary fabric, which you don't want. So get, or produce, a blunt-pointed knife.

Industrial waste-cloth comes in bales; the nearest garage will tell you where to buy it locally. It's cheap and unhandsome, but soft and absorbent and only needs to be hacked into towel-sized sections. It costs a dickens of a lot less than anything else you can buy for the purpose, and works as well or better. (If you positively haven't space in the cellar for a bale, get plain cheesecloth in whatever amount you can store.)

As for jars. You'll need two plastic refrigerator-jars, or freezer-jars. You know what I mean. Your local grocery sells them, and your own refrigerator is likely full of them. They hold a half-pint; they're wide and shallow; and they have nice tight-fitting covers. You'll also need a lot of little jars, holding about two ounces. These can be gathered, for free, by asking your colleagues for empty cold-cream, hand-cream or powder-base jars; if your fellow librarians take no care of their skins, nail the Art Department for empty poster-paint jars.

The wire suede-brush costs ten cents at any shoe-shine emporium. It is essential because, although you and your assistants always wash out brushes, your colleagues don't. They creep in when you aren't looking and fix an ear-ring or a shoe or something with the plastic adhesive (the stuff will fix anything and word gets around) and they don't clean the brush. So you need the wire brush. It works beautifully. Just soak the solidly stiff brush for a while, and then scrub it against the wire bristles. Good as new! (But you can still scowl at your thoughtless colleagues.)

The waxed paper should be cut into halves, thus producing sheets which are just big enough to protect an ordinary-sized page, and which when folded once are perfect to protect hinges or tipped-in pages.

Household wax is that stuff you melt down to cover home-made jellies and jams. Carve the blocks into inch-square chunks. (A candle--a white candle, natch, cut into inch-long sections, is almost as good.) You'll be using it a lot, so the household wax is apt to be more economical.

Finally, wrapping paper. If you intend to do a good deal of re-backing, it will probably pay you to buy a full-sized roll, since it won't deteriorate and can, of course, be used for other odd jobs around the place. In any case, whether you purchase a little or a lot, the next step is to prepare strips about a foot long and something over an inch wide. (The measurements needn't be micrometer-exact, since you will have to trim each individual strip to fit the book on which you will use it; it will even be an advantage to have strips of slightly varying widths and lengths.) If you have the luxury of a paper-cutter, these

Where, What and How Much?   15

strips can be prepared in a few minutes. Simply cut off a section a foot long, the width of the roll, and chop off the strips in a jiffy. With scissors, the job takes longer, since if you haven't a very steady eye you may find it necessary to rule guide-lines. Still another method, which is somewhat quicker than the scissors, is to use a ruler and an Exacto-knife (which is a gadget well known to the makers of model planes; it consists of a razor-sharp replaceable blade fitted into a holder, and most hardware stores carry it. Watch your fingers!) However you produce your supply of strips, store them in the box with the waxed paper.

It is also possible to use, instead of plain strips, a roll of gummed wrapping-paper tape from which you can cut as much as you want for each book. This isn't quite as satisfactory as plain paper, but it is a time-saver.

Mark you, we haven't spent much yet. Dat ole davvil budget has scarcely been nicked. But now come things which must be purchased from one or other of the library supply houses:

- plastic adhesive
- two brushes
- permanent mending tape (for torn pages)
- bone folder
- book cloth
- hinge tape

Once again, foot-notes on each of the above.

The principal variation between brands of the plastic adhesive lies in the viscosity of the dilution--some, that is, have more water in them than others. From experience, we judge that a viscosity of about 1400 cps is about right (and the glossary will explain this rather mystic term for you.) This permits the making of two dilutions, as we shall presently explain. The salesman ought to be able to tell you the viscosity of his brand.

I'd suggest also that you try to get it in a jar or bottle with a narrowish top--somewhere between a half inch and an inch in diameter. This allows you to pour easily and to stop pouring quickly; a wide-mouthed jar tends to spill out a lot more than you want, which is wasteful and disconcerting. Polyethelene containers are much more satisfactory than glass-and-metal.

NOTE: The applicator jar-top seems to be an experiment noble in purpose but not much practical use. It clogs. No matter what, it clogs. And even if it didn't, there are very few ways in which you can usefully employ such a gadget. A brush is much more satisfactory. Moreover, the use of the plastic just as it comes from the bottle or jar, while all right in an emergency, is distinctly extravagant. You get much more mileage out of a quart when the plastic adhesive is properly diluted for various purposes, and what's more, it does a much better job.

Another point to remember is that some, at least, of the plastic adhesives are enormously sensitive to freezing. In some cases the stuff curdles; in others, it forms a solid cake which can't be thawed out; it just sits in the jar and leers at you. So you'll be careful where you store your supply in wintertime, and perhaps lay in enough for the cold weather so as to avoid the possibility of damage in shipping.

The brushes: one should be about ten inches long, with bristles about three-quarters of an inch across and about an inch in length, and proportionately thick. These bristles must be well-set; they take a beating; a little extra expenditure here is good long-range economy.

Where, What and How Much?

The second brush should be a small, tapered brush with a slim handle at least seven inches long. The type of brush used for water-color painting does excellently, provided the bristles are very securely set.

Transparent tape for mending page tears is comparatively new on the market. It looks opaque in the roll, but is almost invisible on the page, and seems to be immune to bleeding, cracking and turning yellow. A dispenser-holder for it is of course a pleasant addition.

A bone folder is a bone folder. It is also known as a folding bone. Neither name is much help if you don't know what it is. It is described in catalogues as an eight-inch piece of laminated composition with blunt edges and rounded ends; it was presumably designed by some unsung genius who had acquired blisters while folding form letters by hand. It is quite indispensable, and don't let anyone tell you that the back of a ruler or the handle of a scissors will take its place. Get a bone folder. If you can possibly manage it, get it in a bright color--since by its inconspicuous flat shape it tends to become practically invisible among the litter of repair work, and thus get thrown away quite easily.

Book-cloth is of various kinds, at various prices, in various forms.
Sometimes it appears in rolls, with stickum on it.
It can also be bought in bolts, quite innocent of stickum but decidedly unwieldy to handle.
It would be ideal if it could be bought in unstuck-up rolls, wouldn't it?
Ah, well.

The least expensive type of book-cloth is shiny, handsome, colorful, and calculated to tint a borrower like a rainbow if he gets caught in the rain. It is not a good investment.

Then there are various grades of water-proof book-cloth, some looking a little like linen, some rather like leather, and some like what they are, which is plastic-impregnated fabric. They're all serviceable and goodlooking, and your choice among them will be dictated simply by your budget and your personal taste. One thing you ought to remember, though, is that the book-cloth you select should provide a good surface for marking. (Fig. 7).

Figure 7

Presumably you've already discovered the water-proof white ink on the market, which when used on waterproof book-cloth does away with the need for protective lacquer or shellac; but on some types of impregnated fabric this ink, due to chemical compatibility, doesn't work so well. Similarly, pens and even a stylus seldom mark comfortably on a heavily grained surface. So it will be wise to ask for a sample of various book-cloth grades and try marking by your preferred method before you make your choice.

NOTE: There are libraries which still feel it is economical to buy the cheaper, non-water-proof book-cloth and protect it from the rain with lacquer or shellac. This theory deserves a fresh examination. To start with, lacquer or shellac is expensive in itself, and while you must of necessity use it on new books, it ups the cost of a re-backed book by a certain amount and about evens out to the cost of water-proof cloth to begin with. On top of that, it takes time to apply, and the drying books take up a whale of a lot of space. Now that it's possible to use water-proof ink, a stylus, or

Where, What and How Much? 19

even the very new pressure-tape gilt, the whole process of re-backing a book becomes a matter of minutes rather than hours, and the resulting saving of time and space justifies a small increase in the amount spent on materials.

Once you've chosen and bought your book-cloth, you'll treat it just as you did the brown paper. That is, you'll cut off a twelve-inch strip the width of the bolt and carve this strip into sections four inches wide. These strips go into the box with the brown paper strips and the waxed paper. Once again, the paper-cutter is a boon. If you haven't one, this is where the red pencil comes in; it shows up much better than ordinary graphite on dark-colored book-cloth. If you intend to do a lot of over-sized juveniles, you'll also provide yourself with a number of strips fourteen inches long and three inches wide.

The last item on our list is hinge-tape.

And here we pause to ponder a problem. It *is* a problem, even a puzzlement.

We could even go so far as to say a pain-in-the-neck.

There's plenty of it on the market. It varies from passable to poor, with a few specimens of plain awful.

There is a reason for this.

To explain it, we ought first to consider what the ideal hinge-tape should be.

- it should be light but tough
- it ought not to ravel at the edges
- it ought not to stretch much when wet, or yet shrink as it dries
- it ought not to be a staring white, since most endpapers are either tinted to start with or have achieved an off-white shade with use
- it ought to have a little "give" to it so as to make a flexible hinge
- finally, it ought to be capable of being stitched together to make a double-hinge without puckering or tending to split along the stitching

It does not yet exist in any catalogue that I know of, but someday a salesman, wearing an outsize halo, will pass by with such a hinge-tape. Keep a red carpet and a ba'ar-trap handy for that splendid day.

What's presently available, as of this writing, is gummed cloth of various kinds. The gum was put on the cloth long before the plastic adhesive was invented, and it's still there because if they left it off, the cloth would ravel at the edges. The gum, stickum, goo or whatever it is tends naturally to dry out (and also, in some disastrous instances, develops a fragrance similar to the city dump on a hot day.)

True, you can ignore the stickum and use the plastic adhesive as if the tape were plain, but the results are not altogether satisfactory. There's not enough "give" to the hinge; it looks fine but there is danger that as it stiffens in drying it will detach the first or last signatures from the contents. It's hard to shape the inner flap of the hinge to the "ledge" of the signatures, which is essential for a good and lasting job. The tape is just too rigid, thanks to

Where, What and How Much?

that stickum, and in the plain awful cases, it cracks apart along the center in no time at all.

Life is hard indeed for menders. But if you are a perfectionist, and can borrow a sewing-machine periodically, you can construct your own hinge-tape without too much trouble.

You'll need, first, plain cloth strips an inch wide, which will hereafter be referred to as "plain hinge tape." Get a light-weight percale; batiste is a little too flimsy and regular sheeting a trifle too heavy. You can either prepare these strips in the same way as you cut the brown paper, or you can cut a continuous strip as long as you like and roll it up. Simpler, if slightly more expensive, is the purchase of surgical gauze bandage--since books can't very well get lockjaw, you can purchase this unsterilized and wholesale at a considerable saving. If you do very little mending, or have plenty of money to spend, you'll find light-weight woven dress-maker tape even more satisfactory.

Next, you prepare "stitched hinge tape". This consists of two strips of cloth, bandage, tape or whatever material you have selected, laid one on top of the other and stitched together down the center. The strips should be an inch-and-a-half wide. Half an hour's work at a sewing-machine will easily produce an ample supply of this harmless-looking but enormously versatile hinge, and once you've discovered the miracles you can accomplish with its use, you won't grudge the time and effort involved.

There is also, as you possibly know, on the market a product called "Double-stitch Binder." This consists of two strips of cloth sewn together one half inch from either margin. The stitching thus creates hinges on either side, while the strip of double cloth between the stitching is supposed to fit neatly over the backs-of-the-signatures and thus replace the "super." It's an ingenious notion.

My objection to it--apart from the fact that it comes with some sort of stickum on it and is thus open to all the objections already made to such hinge material--is that you have to have a tremendous investment bound up in the stuff. You are supposed to keep on hand enough of it, in graduated sizes, so that you'll be able to fit every book perfectly. This can run into money. Moreover, anything with stickum on it doesn't store very well, even under ideal conditions, as if they ever existed in a library supply closet. The less-often-used sizes therefore tend to dry out and crack, or in damp weather get to smelling not much like roses.

Moreover, even though the sizes are carefully graded in eighths of an inch, it's often impossible to get a really perfect fit. The exact fit of a hinge, as we shall presently see, is vital if the book is to stand handling. It's much more satisfactory to attach each hinge separately, rather than to try to accommodate arbitrary section of cloth to backs-of-signatures which may be even a sixteenth of an inch wider or narrower.

There's a simple expedient, though, by which you can use the stuff quite successfully. Just cut it down the middle. This immediately creates what we have called "stitched hinge" and the two strips can be used on any book of any size. We have thus used up quite a lot of the stuff which had begun to deteriorate and obviously wasn't going to be able to wait around for a book which it would fit.

NOTE: It occurs to me that someone is going to pipe up--some new mender who hasn't been through the mill--with an inquiry about paper hinges. They're neat and simple and inexpensive; why not use them?

Where, What and How Much?

The answer is equally neat and simple. Now that we have the plastic adhesive, there's no need or excuse for a hinge <u>inside</u> the contents of the book. To attach the contents to the casing, cloth is necessary because cloth is at once permanent and removable.

A paradox.

Thusly: if you use paper, it will presently split. You put another strip of paper over it. <u>That</u> splits. Your next strip of paper will create so much bulk that the contents will simply bulge right out of the casing, and in addition, you have a book which no bindery will touch with a ten-foot pole.

But it is always possible to remove a cloth hinge, even when it has been put in with the plastic adhesive. It ain't easy, mind you, but it can be done. So, practically speaking, you can put in new hinges indefinitely, so long as they are cloth. But in fact, if the hinge-tape is sufficiently flexible and is put in properly, you very likely won't have to replace it within the lifetime of an ordinary book.

So there we are, completely outfitted with supplies for everything but the most complicated and unusual repairs, and yet everything will fit on a small shelf or even into a fairly deep drawer. The time we've expended in preparing these supplies will now pay dividends a dozen times over, since we can start to work at a moment's notice. Used as I shall now direct, this arsenal will produce results guaranteed to dazzle your colleagues and utterly outwit your most energetic borrowers.

Chapter Four
A NECESSARY PARENTHESIS
WHICH YOU REALLY SHOULDN'T SKIP

This *is* necessary, honest.

So curb your natural impatience to get on with the delightful business of mending.

Right here we stop to consider who is going to do the repairs.

Menders seem to fall, or subside, into three groups.

There is the librarian who has been mending, as a sideline, all her lengthy career; when she retires from actively pursuing the elusive borrower, she often stays on part-time to mend. She is very nice; I know lots of her; don't bother to give her this book. She's perfectly happy with her own ways and you're very lucky to have her. Don't go fretting her with this new-fangled stuff.

Then there is the full-fledged professional staff member who gets mending because somebody has to do it. Some of these, like myself, get fascinated by the job, and to their inspired suggestions from all across the country many of the ideas in this book are due. Others remain immune and unhappy, waiting as patiently as possible for the day when somebody new gets hired onto whom they can dump the job. It's just possible that some of these, if trapped or badgered into reading this, will catch fire. I sort of hope so. You don't know what you're missing, kids.

Thirdly, mending is done by paid pages, or by unpaid

part-time volunteers. Their work is necessarily supervised by a staff mender, and that staff mender ought to be able to mend at least as well as they, and give more constructive thought to it.

In any case, the person in charge of mending (and I use the feminine pronoun without the slightest wish to suggest that there aren't male librarians who are very good indeed at book repair; in fact, they're mostly too good at it to need a book on the subject) whether she has a whole crew of assistants or operates on her own, has the responsibility of ordering supplies, judging the new materials on the market, trying out new techniques, experimenting with new ideas, and keeping a beady eye on the ball--the ball being a term for the nice balance between not spending too much money and equally not letting a single worth-while book escape from the collection. It is a responsibility. A good mender not only saves money (a useful thing in itself) but she also preserves the collection, which is far more important. There's a good deal of pride and pleasure involved.

There are also headaches--minor but definite.

If your menders are teen-agers, whether paid or volunteer, you've got to figure on certain natural phenomena. Kids mostly are deft, clever and ingenious, and once they've been carefully trained, it pays to give them considerable lee-way to improvise on special problems. They'll often surprise you with their excellent notions. On the other hand, in the spring they'll tend to put in the contents up-side-down every so often, or use purple backing on a pink book, or carefully tip in a detached signature backside-to. Don't blow your stack. You worried about spring proms yourself.

WHICH YOU REALLY SHOULDN'T SKIP 27

If your menders are full-grown women being civic-minded, budget enough of your own time to finish the mending when necessary. Children and husbands tend to take precedence over book-repair, and who shall say they shouldn't? Just be prepared.

Finally, cultivate Ukridge's big, broad, flexible outlook. Anything can be done better than it is being done, anytime. I'm positive that everything I suggest here can be improved upon; I hope it will be; mending is anything but static. It's adventurous and amusing and if another edition of this (heaven send!) is needed, it'll undoubtedly have to be rewritten from scratch. And right here perhaps I can remind you again that if you have already dreamed up improvements and would like to share them, I'll be more than grateful to hear from you.

A word about ordering supplies. It often looks like a satisfactory economy to order a lot of something and take a discount. Just be careful to note that some materials keep better than others. Brown paper stores admirably; book-cloth does within reason; anything with stickum on it does not; plastic adhesive mustn't be frozen, and in general seems to be better for rather frequent re-ordering rather than lengthy storage in a supply closet which may not be ideal for the purpose.

That supply closet, in fact, will determine your purchasing very substantially, or should. If pipes run through it, or if it's in a damp cellar, or if one wall abuts on the side of the building, you may decide not to store much of anything over a long period of time. But if--this is rare--it is properly warm and dry at all seasons, you can keep a greater quantity of almost anything on hand.

But against this, you must weigh the possibility that at any moment, as I have said, somebody may come up with a nice new miracle, and if you have two year's supply of whatever-it-is already bought, you're stuck with it. Try to balance your ordering between day-to-day needs and long-term planning. You don't want to be at the mercy of suppliers who give you that, "So sorry, we're fresh out, we'll have it for you in a couple of months" routine. But equally, when the day comes that something new and good turns up and you pine to start using it at once, what'll you do with that closet full of stuff that's got to be used up? (You could, I suppose, auction off extra percale to married members of the staff to make pillow-cases.) You observe that ordering takes a good deal of intelligent forethought. That's part of your job.

Chapter Five
TIME AND MOTION
or
We, Too, Can Be Efficiency Engineers

At last, we are about to mend.

But wait.

<u>What</u> are we going to mend?

Books, you say. And you say truly. But are we just going to reach at random into a pile of ragged objects and pick out a plum, which may need any one of seven possible repairs?

We are not going to do anything of the kind--not if we are as smart as I think menders are. Efficient book repair starts long before we pick up a brush. It starts right at the receiving desk, and to prove it, with your indulgence, we'll consider for a minute or two the business of sorting.

You and your colleagues, as you check the incoming books, naturally put aside any book which seems to have anything at all the matter with it. Now your colleagues are probably not menders, and while they are quite capable of noticing a strip of bacon used as a bookmark, or observing that the contents has fallen out of its covers, they may very well not be up on the more subtle forms of disintegration. Therefore it must be part of your job to train your fellow-workers to recognize the very first indication of trouble, because if they will be unfailingly severe about this, you--and the collection--will be saved an enormous amount of wear-and-tear. If you have--as I trust--a sympathetic Front Office, you may be allowed to demonstrate at a staff meeting, and thereafter to indoctrinate new members of the staff as they come along. It is bad business to allow a book to go out "just one more time" and it will pay you to kick and scream until this point is firmly tattooed on your colleagues' memory.

The harvest, then, which is reaped at the receiving desk comes to you. You, as the expert, go over this pile of miscellaneous problems. You will find that about half of them fall into two groups, both very easy to fix, and both discussed in the next chapter. It would be foolish to keep them hanging around for a week or more, when they can be put back into circulation in a matter of minutes. So you will commandeer shelf space, or even floor space, and make two piles. In the first will be books which have worked loose in their spines; in the second, books whose end-papers have detached themselves and need only be fastened back where they came from. (This will be crystal clear when you have read the following chapter.)

A third pile will contain books which need real operational mending. If you have space, these can be separated again into those which need hinges and those which need new spines. (Replacing a worn spine is technically known as "backing" a book.) Quite often a book will need both, so it will go first into the "mending" pile and then, when it is once more whole and intact, into the "backing" pile for further work. (You may also need a corner in which to hide really frightful

We, Too, Can Be Efficiency Engineers

problems until you have time to deal with them.)

In addition to these categories, there are the books which have torn pages, or whose plastic protective covers need fixing, or need to be erased, or must be washed after contact with a sticky-fingered infant. There will be few of these on any given day, and if they can be sequestered handily, they can be taken care of in a jiffy in a spare moment.

This assembly-line technique allows the mender to put stray moments to good use, and after all, Time is your biggest problem, isn't it? Without this type of sorting, the mender has to have all sorts of stuff instantly available, or waste time looking for it, and she must keep shifting gears as she works--now washing a book, next putting on a back, then getting out the tape to fix a torn page. Properly, she should sit down prepared to do a batch of mending of one particular type, with everything she needs for it ready at hand, and whip the project through as speedily as if a time-and-motion engineer had studied the job for her.

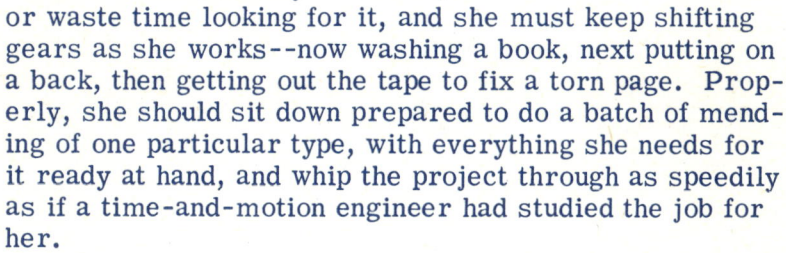

This planned sorting makes it quite superfluous to put little notes into each book, pointing out what needs to be done to it. If it's in the backing pile, it needs a back, and that's that. Even a fourteen-year-old can grasp that elementary point. Yet even you yourself, if you do the mending without a smidgin of help, will be grateful if, when you sit down to mend, you can reach for a pile of books all of which need the same treatment, which you are prepared to give them without further fuss or bother.

Chapter Six
EASY DOES IT
or
Two for the Money

We're off!

We've cleared a table space, spread out old newspapers upon it, and upon these laid a stack of old newspaper torn into fourths, so that as each piece of paper becomes sticky we can discard it for a fresh one. We have brought out our brushes, bone, scissors, jars, and a chunk of soft waste-cloth or cheesecloth. We also bring out the box in which we store brown paper, waxed paper and bookcloth strips, although we will only need the waxed paper in this chapter. And we have our piece of wax. (We won't need it for any operation in this chapter, but we are thinking ahead. Each time we open a book for mending, we run an exploratory finger over any hinge which has been previously inserted, just to see if it is still well waxed. Sometimes, in very hot weather, or if a book has been stored on somebody's radiator, the wax may wear a bit thin. It scarcely takes a second to run another coat of wax over it, and so that's what we do. We've gone into the reasons for waxing, so this is just a reminder that even for this very simple first excursion into mending, the wax is a handy thing to keep by you.)

Now we must prepare the plastic adhesive.

First, we will prepare LIGHT DILUTION.

(Actually, we don't need both dilutions, LIGHT and HEAVY, for this chapter. But it's more convenient to describe them both at once, so that you can see how they differ. For the purposes of this chapter, HEAVY DILUTION would be sufficient.)

For LIGHT DILUTION, pour an inch of plastic adhesive into one of the refrigerator jars. Add to it the contents of one of your small two-ounce jars, of water. If you insist on being finical, you can invest in a kitchen measuring cup marked with ounces, but actually all these measurements are approximate. The viscosity of your chosen brand, the state of the weather and especially the humidity, all alter slightly the amount of water you add. What you wish to get is a dilution which is not watery-thin, but spreads freely and dries to a thin, transparent glaze. With a little practice and experiment, you will quickly get the "feel" of the right dilution and adjust your mixture by a few teaspoons of water one way or the other. The plastic adhesive will stick even in a very thin dilution indeed; all you want to avoid is a solution so thin that the water soaks the paper to which it is applied too much, so that the paper wrinkles or tears.

Use the larger of the two brushes to stir, (and remember to put the brush into a small jar of water afterwards!)

Next, HEAVY DILUTION.

Into the second refrigerator jar pour another inch of plastic adhesive, and add exactly half as much water as you added for LIGHT DILUTION.

This matter of dilutions is especially tricky. For one thing, the plastic adhesive is still in the experimental stage, and it often happens that one batch from a supplier will differ considerably in viscosity, not to mention other respects, from the previous order from the same supplier. They're trying to improve it, you see, and more power to them for it. None the less, it'll be wise for you to ask your salesman about the viscosity rating of his product, so that if the viscosity is less than in the one you have been using, you can add proportionately less water. An adhesive with a viscosity rating of about 1400 cps seems the most economical, but if you choose a product with a lower rating, simply adjust your dilution to match. A little experiment will make this problem easy to solve.

The point of making dilutions at all? Well, there are several points, really. The plastic adhesive, usually, as it comes from jar or bottle, is rather thick for easy spreading with a brush. You have to dip often and brush hard; thinned, a single sweep of the brush covers a surface for a hinge, and the dilution sticks just as well. Next, the plastic adhesive when used in its original form tends to be difficult during hot spells or rainy weather; it soaks through the cloth of the hinge and in spite of our vigorous waxing, sticks together with itself when the book is closed. LIGHT DILUTION is much less apt to do this. Thirdly, dipping the brush into the supply jar can be expensive. It's possible to have a slightly discolored or dirty brush without noticing it, and when this is dipped into your main supply, you ruin a whole jar or bottle for future use.

These are all reasonable arguments for making dilutions. The added fact that by so doing you save money and get a lot more books mended out of a given jar is just another point, and not the most important, but also not to be ignored, either.

Let's get on.

If you have bought yourself jars of different colors, this will distinguish one dilution from the other. If not, label each clearly.

Put waxed paper over the top of each refrigerator jar and replace the covers lightly--that is, don't press them home. (There is a form of clear plastic wrapping familiar to housewives, which can be washed and used again-- you probably use it yourself to wrap left-overs in the refrigerator--and which is infinitely preferable to plain waxed paper for protecting the tops of our jars. An investment in a few sheets of this stuff will give a good deal of satisfaction.)

We will now take three solemn vows:

- Never to leave a brush out of water when it is not in use

- Never to dip a wet brush into either dilution without first drying it on the piece of waste-cloth so handily placed beside the water-jar (because if we do, the dilution will shortly become much too thin)

- Never to leave the waxed paper (or whatever we use for protection) and the covers off the containers when we go to answer the phone or gossip with a favorite borrower, or even when we aren't using that particular dilution for an appreciable length of time (because if we do, the stuff will skin over and thicken up)

Two For the Money

Cross your heart and hope to die? All right then, let's get on.

In the normal course of events--puppy dogs and floods excepted--the first thing that happens to a book is that the glue which holds the contents into the casing begins to crack and dry just where the cheesecloth hinge--remember?--is folded into the edge of the spine. Got a new book handy? Open it, holding each side-cover out like a wing, and let the contents hang free. Properly, unless your new book is very poorly made or has been warehoused for quite a time, the contents will fit cozily up into the spine, with just a narrow tunnel of light between the spine itself and the backs of the signatures.

But now find yourself a newish novel which has circulated maybe three times, and hold it up in the same fashion. (Fig. 8). Where's the contents now? It hangs forward, suspended by the cheesecloth-and-end-papers, and you could almost drive a truck through the gap between the spine and the backs of the signatures. I've known this to happen before a book circulated at all. The cause is the drying out of the narrow line of glue which originally held the ledge up into the curve of the spine--which obviously suggests the cure.

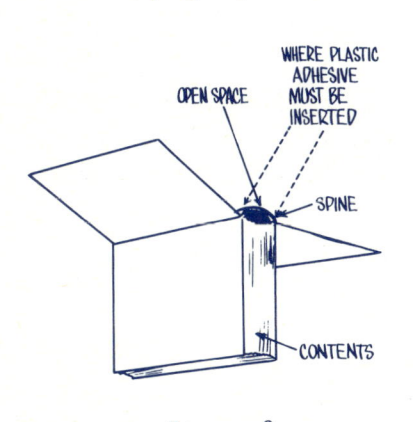

Figure 8

If you can train your colleagues to catch every book at this point, so that you can fix it immediately, you'll almost work yourself right out of a job--as mender, that is.

Now some misguided souls will tell you--they <u>have</u> told you, because I've seen it in black-and-white--that the cure is to pour or squirt plastic adhesive down the back of the signatures and plaster the spine firmly against their surface. A horrible thought. Don't do it.

(NOTE: Why not? Because if books were intended to be made that way, that's how they'd be made. In fact, the play between the backs of the signatures and the spine is vitally important. It permits the book to be opened and closed innumerable times without the spine cracking. Take a new book, open it, and see how the spine curves outward, preserving its shape and contour. Then, if you are still skeptical, try gluing a spine onto the backs of the signatures and then open the book. See how the spine cracks and folds, trying to accommodate itself to the movement? After a few weeks of such stress, the spine has lost its lettering and is just a limp, sorry piece of cloth. I learned this the hard way, but there's no reason why you should.)

Instead, fold the side-covers back and pull the contents as far forward as it will come without resistance. (It can happen that the glue has loosened only on one side, or at the top on both sides but not at the bottom, or in various combinations of these possibilities. The most usual case is that the contents has come loose entirely, the full length of the spine, but you can easily adjust your treatment to less spectacular cases.)

Take your small brush, and dip the HANDLE into the jar of HEAVY DILUTION. Run the handle down the inside of the spine, right at the very edge, which will be precisely under the groove or crease which marks the juncture of the spine and the side-covers. Be careful not to get any plastic adhesive onto the backs of the signatures or the inside of the spine, but be sure that the inside of the hinge is well-coated.

Reverse the book in your grip, so that the bottom is upwards, and do the same thing.

Close the book firmly, pressing the contents up where they belong into the curve of the spine. Take your bone and run it heavily along the creases on either side of the spine. Look to see if this has caused any of the plastic adhesive to ooze out onto the edges of the pages at top or bottom; if so, wipe it away with your cloth.

Set the book aside to dry.

Open it again, once more holding it by the side-covers like wings, and observe that the contents once more fit up comfortably and securely into the spine, yet there is ample play between the spine and the backs of the signatures. In fact, it is a much sturdier book than when you bought it, and will last much longer. Put it back into circulation with a pleased smile.

I trust you've remembered to wipe off the brush handle?

If not, you must be pretty sticky by now and had better pause to wash up.

NOTE: Books, to be frank about it, are not very clean. Why librarians don't come down with every known disease in the medical dictionaries I'll never know. It casts some doubt on the germ theory, doesn't it? Anyway, library books are frequently unlovely. Either they have accumulated dust for twenty years in the stacks, or they have suffered unconscionable adventures out among the public. So, when you work on or with them, your hands get dirty. ("It must be so pleasant to work in a library--so clean and quiet!") You'll find it wise, as a mender, to wash often. Otherwise you'll find the plastic adhesive taking your fingerprints down to posterity with a clarity which the FBI would love. The stuff washes off quite easily unless you let it set for several hours, owing to the oil in your skin. It will _not_ wash off your clothes if you spill it, so a smock is a sensible precaution.

The next thing to happen to a book, if the above repair isn't made in time, is the separation of the end-papers (and whatever extraneous sheets have been glued to them) from the first or last signatures of the contents. (Fig. 9). It's usually a perfectly clean separation, showing the cheesecloth underneath, and if you look closely, you'll see traces of the glue or paste which originally held the end-papers down along the "ledge." If you don't know how a book is made, this separation looks quite terrifying.

In the old days, it was customary to slap a paper hinge over this gaping crack, with lamentable results.

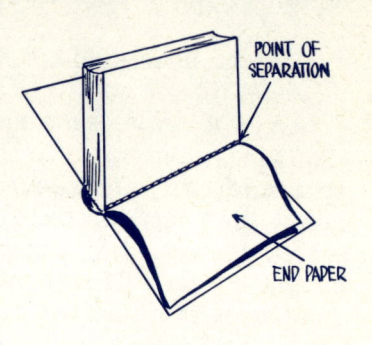

Figure 9

Got a fairly new book handy? Try giving the end-papers a sturdy tweak, and see what happens.

The cure is simple.

Open the book to the place where the separation has occurred (it will often be at the real title page in front, and at the last printed page in back.) Using the small brush again, but in orthodox fashion this time--the brush-end, not the handle--carefully paint the "ledge" with HEAVY DILUTION. Make sure you don't get any plastic adhesive on the rest of the page, although any that leaks through onto the cheesecloth is all to the good. Fold a piece of waxed paper and lay the fold just beyond the point where you left off painting--this will be anywhere from an eighth of an inch to a quarter of an inch from the inner edge of the page, depending on the size of the book and the width of the "ledge."

Now close the end-paper down onto the contents, and use your bone to firm it solidly into place along the "ledge."

Finally, close the side-cover and run your bone along the crease beside the spine.

When it has dried, the book will be ready to meet the world again, much stronger than before.

NOTE: Drying times vary. As I have explained, the plastic adhesive is extremely sensitive to the weather. On a clear, brisk day with low humidity, the stuff will dry almost while you look at it--half an hour is surely ample. But in humid weather, or during a rainy spell, you'll have to extend the drying period considerably. Don't get mad. If it weren't for this weather-sensitivity, the plastic adhesive wouldn't be the flexible miracle that it is. In the worst of weather --fog, drizzle, hot and sweltering--over-night should do it.)

And there, if you catch your books in time, is half your mending problem solved. These two simple operations will keep new books looking new for an astonishing length of time. Thus correctly repaired at the start of their career, they should go for several years without the need of extensive mending. Try to drum this into the heads of your colleagues, so that they will exercise the strictest attention in their examination of in-coming books.

Chapter Seven
SMALL FRY
or
Odds and Ends for Spare Moments

Before we go on to more complicated techniques, we may as well attend to those minor repairs which turn up erratically.

MARKED-UP PAGES

Pencil marks require an art-gum, naturally.

Regular ink marks, whether scrawled by Junior or carefully underlined by a scholar whom you hope flunks his course, can be removed with ink eradicator. You can even use household bleach (sodium hypochloride) diluted half-and-half with water. Just be sure you don't take the text out, too. Apply tenderly with a soft cloth and don't rub hard.

Ball-point ink is there to stay, until science discovers a bleach for it.

Crayon (bless the little fiends) cannot be altogether removed. There is a product newly on the market which will remove about ninety percent of wax crayon marks, leaving only a faintly colored blur. (You'll find it advertised in the trade papers.) Juvenile departments should consider it a useful investment.

TORN PAGES

The new permanent mending tape on the market solves the problem of torn pages effectively and quickly. The only thing to remember about it is that it isn't quite as easy to use as it looks. You must lay the strip of tape exactly where you intend it to go the first time; otherwise you'll find that the adhesive surface has picked up the print like magic. With a little practice and a steady hand, however, this almost invisible tape mends a page beautifully and, as far as several years' experience indicates, for keeps.

Just for the record, we will note that there are other ways of mending torn pages, though they both take so much more time and result in so much less satisfaction that it's hard to see why anyone nowadays would care.

First, if the tear is "feathered"--that is, a real tear and not a clean cut--it is possible to fix it with the plastic adhesive. Lay the torn page on an underlying sheet of waxed paper, carefully anoint the edges of the tear with **HEAVY DILUTION**, using the small brush, and fit the edges of the tear together. Smooth down gently with a crumpled bit of waxed paper, overlay with another smooth sheet of waxed paper, and close the book to dry.

Second, for either a tear or a cut, use onion-skin paper. Proceed as above for a "feathered" tear, but lay over the tear after it has been fitted together a strip of onion-skin about an inch wide. Smooth down firmly and allow to dry. When thoroughly dry, with your fingers pull the onion skin sharply away from the page. Enough paper will adhere to the point of the tear to hold it together quite securely.

But I repeat, why bother?

LOOSE PAGES

A single page which has come loose can be tipped in very easily.

Open the book widely at the point where the page has fallen out. Using the small brush and **HEAVY DILUTION**, run a delicate line of plastic adhesive down the very bottom of the trough between the pages, trying not to coat more than a sixteenth of an inch of the pages on either side. Fold a piece of waxed paper close down beside the right-hand page. Fit the loose page firmly back into the space between the pages, making sure it is straight and properly aligned with the top and bottom of the contents. Fold another sheet of waxed paper and slip it down between the inserted page and the left-hand page of the contents. Close the book and allow to dry.

This same procedure, using slightly more of the plastic adhesive, permits the insertion of loose plates, illustrations, diagrams, maps and so forth.

This same technique is used when the center two pages of a signature tear loose from their stitching. These central pages will of course be one page, folded in the middle; they are replaced exactly as if they were a single page.

But it may happen that a whole signature will come loose--often the first or last signature in the book. Here the stitching has broken and perhaps eight folded sheets come out all at once. They can be tipped in, one inside the other, as if they were individual pages, but this is not recommended. A slightly more complicated procedure is far more lasting and satisfactory.

Thus: put the signature together as it was in the beginning, and observe that at the fold there are punched holes through which the original stitching ran. Get a needle and white thread--#20 if you have it, or #40 doubled--and sew the signatures together through these convenient holes. (Fig. 10). Leave a couple of inches of thread at the bottom of the fold, and another couple of inches at the top. Fold these thread-ends under the signature and lay the newly-sewn signature back into its place, which you have anointed with plastic adhesive just as if the signature were a single page. This, which scarcely takes a couple of minutes, actually reconstructs the book as it was and adds neither bulk nor future problems. (This job arises so seldom that you needn't invest in needle-and-thread as a permanent supply. Just borrow them when required from that useful member of the staff who always has them on hand when a hem comes down or a button drops off.)

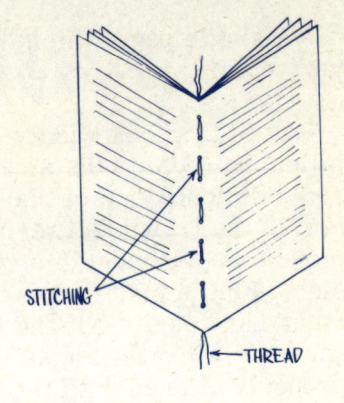

Figure 10

WASHING A BOOK

If the book is protected by a transparent plastic cover, it's a simple matter to wipe it clean with a damp cloth.

But if you are dealing with the original cloth binding, or a rebound book, you must remember to work quickly and with a clean cloth wrung out almost dry. Any mild soap will do, or you can invest in any of the patented detergent cleaners sold for the purpose. The main thing is not too much water. Keep turning the cloth to maintain a clean surface, work briskly but lightly; and remember that the water which inevitably soaks into the cloth will make the book look much dirtier than it actually is. When it dries, you'll be astonished at how much cleaner it is than you thought. Therefore don't scrub too long. A quick once-over fairly often is more sensible than a prolonged bath when the dirt has become ingrained.

Follow, when dry, with a coat of shellac or lacquer on original covers, especially if they reveal a tendency to bleed.

TRANSPARENT PLASTIC COVERS

The care and repair of these will be suggested by the manufacturer, and you need only follow directions, using whatever techniques he suggests.

LOST OR HOPELESSLY DAMAGED PAGES

If the missing material can be copied onto four pages or less of ordinary type-writer bond, cut to fit the book, it is quite possible to insert these new pages into the place where the loss has occurred.

Type the material, keeping the same margins as the book-page, and put the typed pages in order. Paint plastic adhesive, just as it comes from the bottle, along the inner edges of these grouped pages. Allow to dry. Then insert these new pages, which are now firmly attached to each other, into the book in the same way that you would insert a loose page or plate. It will probably be necessary to trim the new pages after the book is thoroughly dry, so as to bring them precisely into line with the rest of the contents. Use sharp scissors and a steady hand.

The insertion of more than four new pages will be a dangerous strain on the casing, and so it isn't recommended.

Chapter Eight
OPERATING THEATER
or
The Expert to the Rescue

The time comes when a book must be mended in the full sense of the term.

The original glue has dried out. The signatures are beginning to separate. The end-papers are starting to split along the hinge-juncture. One more circulation and the borrower will bring the thing back in a paper bag. And no fault of his, this time. The book is just doin' what comes naturally.

The danger-point--the moment when an expert mender diagnoses the necessity for a drastic operation--is the moment when the end-papers split. Yet there is sometimes an earlier indication, worth watching for, and that's when the signatures begin to separate. This can usually be spotted by up-ending the book, holding the covers out like wings, and looking to see if the signatures are still a solid block or if they have begun to hate each other. For some reason this is most often noticeable at the bottom rather than at the top of the contents.

The minute this happens, the splitting of the end-papers can be expected momentarily.

CASE ONE

  SYMPTOMS: separated signatures, due to drying glue. End-papers still intact.

  CURE: Hold the contents and the back cover in one hand, the front cover in the other. Yank.

The front end-paper will split, but the underlying cheesecloth will simply pull away from the backs of the signatures. Yank again, to see how far the cheesecloth will peel away. Usually it won't come off for more than about half the width of the backs-of-the-signatures. (Fig. 11). (If, in the course of this operation, the cheesecloth splits, you have a CASE TWO on your hands and will proceed as presently directed.)

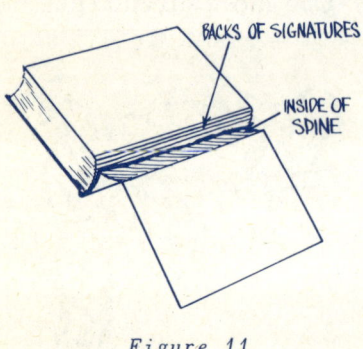

Figure 11

Lay the book down and hold the front cover as far away from the backs of the signatures as possible. Take your larger brush, dip it well into HEAVY DILUTION, and cover as much of the backs-of-the-signatures as you can reach. Don't close the book; set it aside to dry.

When the plastic adhesive is thoroughly dry--you can easily tell; it will look almost transparent and not feel tacky to the touch of a finger--trim the frayed edges of the end-papers carefully and neatly, and attach the front cover to the contents with plain hinge tape.

The method of applying a plain cloth hinge is easily learned, although it is not quite as easy as it looks. Since it is a major technique, we will now describe it carefully.

The Expert to the Rescue

First, cut a length of plain hinge tape the exact length of the contents of the book.

Next, apply LIGHT DILUTION with your larger brush to a half-inch of the first page of the contents--actually this will be the contents-side of the original end-paper--and to half an inch of the side-cover, along the hinge-juncture where the split occurred. Take your hinge tape and lay one half of it along the contents where the plastic adhesive has been applied, fitting it carefully and exactly into the curve of the "ledge." (Fig. 12). Now lift the side-cover and hold it so that the edge of the side-cover exactly meets the top of the "ledge" and smooth the rest of the hinge onto the side-cover. Wait a moment, holding the side-cover in place, so that the plastic adhesive has a chance to "catch." Then carefully smooth the whole hinge, using crumpled waxed paper or your piece of soft cloth, and then use the bone to make sure that the hinge fits precisely down into the curve of the "ledge." Set the book aside, still open to dry for five minutes. (In very wet weather, make it ten minutes.) Then open and close the front cover several times, gently, so that the hinge can make any minute adjustment which is necessary to a perfectly comfortable fit.

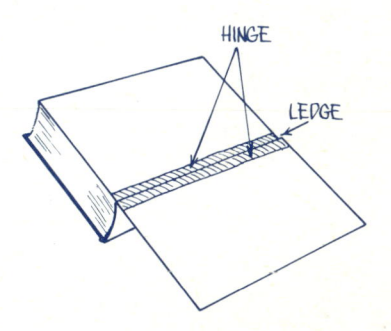

Figure 12

Now fold a piece of waxed paper and slip it between the front cover and the contents, and close the book. Set it aside for twenty minutes (give or take five minutes for weather conditions.) By that time the hinge should be fairly dry and thoroughly secure. Open the front cover again and run your piece of wax vigorously over the entire surface of the hinge, and also over the area of paper next to the hinge on either side, just in case any of the plastic adhesive has leaked or smeared onto the paper.

Naturally, when in due course the back end-paper splits, you will simply follow this same procedure at that point.

These two procedures, which are really much easier to practice than to explain, are often all the repair that the average book requires in a lifetime. If the hinges are put in carefully, with a strict regard for the way a book is made, it's probable that the contents will wear out before it manages to work loose from the casing again.

CASE TWO

>   SYMPTOMS: Front and back end-papers split; cheesecloth either altogether split or beginning to go at either back or front; signatures well separated

>   CURE: We must replace the glue and the cheesecloth, and do this in such a manner that the stress on the casing will be, as far as possible, exactly the same as when the book was made. Obviously a plain cloth hinge will not be sufficient, since the inner leverage of the cheesecloth "super" has been lost. We must replace this effectively if we want to do a lasting job.

This is the book, heaven help it, which during the critical period when a CASE ONE repair would have saved it, was in the hands of an "active borrower." (What do people do with books? Hold batting practice?) Or it may be just a very ancient book which has simply dehydrated on the stack shelf until it cracks apart at a touch.

We will assume that the actual break has occurred at the front of the book, which is much the most usual case.

>   NOTE: Sometimes--not often--the cheesecloth "super" is curiously stubborn. The signatures have separated, the glue is dry, the end-papers have split--

The Expert to the Rescue

but the "super" holds on. In this case, simply slit it with your knife. It is essential to get at the backs of the signatures, or, presently, the whole contents will fall out into your lap.

First, trim off the torn edges of "super" and end-paper neatly, right back to the "ledge" on the contents-side and to the card-board side-cover.

Now fold back the front side cover and spine so that the entire back of the signatures is revealed, (Fig. 13) and scrape away as much of the dried glue as will come off easily. Don't scrape too hard, or you may damage the stitching. (With older books you can scrape like billy-o; pre-world-war-one books were made to stand harsh treatment.)

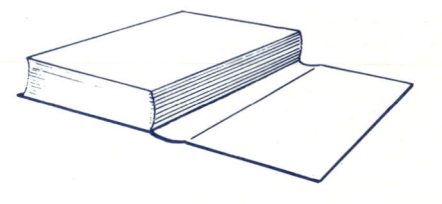

Figure 13

Lay the book on a shelf or table-edge so that the backs-of-the-signatures project about an inch, and anchor the book in place with a couple of heavy books laid on top. (You can, of course, use a book-press if you have one.)

Paint the backs of the signatures thoroughly with **HEAVY DILUTION**, using your larger brush. Lap over slightly onto the front page (which is, of course, one half of the original end-paper) so as to secure it solidly to the contents (in some cases it will have become wholly detached.) Be generous with your application and press the signatures together. Leave to dry.

When the plastic adhesive has become transparent, you'll find that you can lift the whole contents by a single page, and the chances of the signatures separating again are very slim. Now all we need do is put the book back into its casing.

The way in which this can be done with absolutely maximum efficiency and for lasting results is now to be described. It is the second major technique in our bag of tricks, and well worth mastering. Once you have learned it, nothing will dismay you--from a First Folio to one of those enormous bound Patent Office Gazettes.

Cut off a length of stitched hinge-tape the length of the contents.

This stitched hinge-tape, as we know, consists of two inch-and-a-half wide strips of cloth sewn together down the middle. This sewing naturally produces four similar flaps, two on one side of the stitching, two on the other.

We need only three flaps.

That is, we need one flap to attach to the first page of the contents, and a matching flap to attach to the side-cover. The other two flaps must be attached, one on top of the other, to the backs-of-the-signatures. In this way we will create a hinge which derives its strength not only from the plastic adhesive which holds it, but also from the natural strength of the cloth. There will be no strain on the side-cover, and very little on the first signature of the contents; most of the strain will fall on the double-thickness of cloth attached to the backs of the signatures, and this it will be well able to handle.

Putting in this hinge is simplicity itself, but it does require a certain amount of care.

Dip your larger brush in LIGHT DILUTION (which is to be preferred because it will not create problems later on by sticking to the other side of the hinge, and also because you can work more quickly with it than with HEAVY DILUTION) and brush a coat over the backs of the signatures and a further coat over half inch of the first page of the contents. Work quickly and don't mind if you splash over a trifle.

The Expert to the Rescue

Now take up your strip of stitched hinge tape and open out two flaps with your fingers. Fit these two flaps down over the "ledge" so that the stitching comes exactly at the top of the ledge, one flap attaching itself to the front page of the contents, the other fitting down onto the backs-of-the-signatures. Smooth into place carefully. It is vital that the stitching come precisely at the top of the ledge, and this is the thing you must be most careful about.

Wait a moment for the plastic adhesive to "catch" and then paint the flap which lies over the backs-of-the-signatures with a quick application of LIGHT DILUTION. Smooth the flap which neighbors this attached flap down on top of the plastic adhesive and rub it well into place with a bit of crumpled waxed paper. (Fig. 14). Now take your bone and make sure that the flap which is attached to the first page of the contents is comfortably fitted into the curve of the "ledge" since this fit will make a world of difference in the finished job.

Figure 14

Now lay the book aside to dry. Do something else in the meantime.

I know it's a temptation to get on with the job, but don't. If you do, the wet plastic adhesive along the backs-of-the-signatures will catch onto the spine, and you won't like the results. Let the whole thing dry; go and do something else, like another book. You see why an assembly-line technique on a number of similar books pays off?

When, eventually, the plastic adhesive is transparent and the hinge not even tacky, rub wax thoroughly all over the backs-of-the-signatures and the attached double-flap. Thus we avoid trouble in wet weather.

Comes now the final and most critical part of the operation.

We have the contents, the side-cover, and a single flap sticking up along the edge of the ledge. We must put these together. So, paint the edge of the side-cover with **LIGHT DILUTION**.

Very, very carefully, then, fit the side-cover up against the top of the ledge where the stitching is, and smooth the fourth flap down onto the side-cover. (Fig. 15). Use your fingers; God gave them to you for such artistic work. Now, as you did when putting in a plain hinge, lay the book aside for five minutes, open, and then close and open the side cover a few times, gently, to permit the hinge to make whatever minute adjustments may be necessary for a permanently comfortable fit.

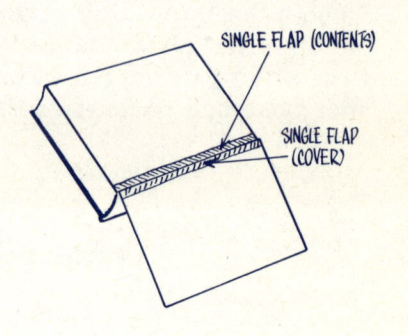

Figure 15

Thereafter, you proceed exactly as for a plain hinge. Insert a folded piece of waxed paper between side-cover and contents, close the book and allow to dry for twenty minutes or so. Open again and wax the whole hinge surface and the neighboring areas of paper. Set the book aside to dry for whatever period seems reasonable, considering the weather.

The results will look good, open comfortably, and be so strong that a brace of Missouri mules won't be able to tear it apart. That's why you must work so care-

The Expert to the Rescue   57

fully and exactly; you can't easily take it apart and start over. (You <u>can</u> do it, if you insist, but it's a difficult and messy job.)

I know that this all sounds dreadfully complicated, but so would a step-by-step exposition of how to eat an ice-cream cone. Actually, as I know from experience, anyone can learn to put in a stitched hinge perfectly after three or four tries. The whole secret is getting the stitching to lie precisely at the top of the "ledge" and matching the side-cover thereto. Otherwise it's a breeze.

Obviously, if a book requires not one hinge but two, you'll put in the front hinge first, let the book dry, and then put in a hinge at the back.

But what, you inquire, if the contents aren't sufficiently bulky to permit two sets of flaps to be attached to the backs-of-the-signatures without overlapping?

A sensible question.

The answer: trim the double-flaps down so that they <u>don't</u> overlap. As little as a quarter of an inch of double-flap will hold securely. If the book is even narrower than that, permit a small overlap--it won't hurt much. In the case of a very, very narrow book, such as a juvenile picture-book, we use a quite different technique which will be explained subsequently.

And now, armed with just these two techniques, you are equipped to face the most battered of books--ignoring special cases which rarely turn up and which will be considered in later chapters. These two techniques, plus the technique of book-backing which comes in the next chapter, are the basis for all modern mending, and once you have learned them you need shrink from nothing. Practice them until you are sure of them--it won't take long--and then settle down to live it up among the paste-brushes; you'll have it made.

Chapter Nine
BACKING UP
or
Why, When and How to Replace a Spine

The next step in mending is the replacement of a torn or damaged, or even just tired, spine--a procedure known technically as "backing" a book.

When should it be done?

Obviously, when the original spine is no longer either legible or attractive, for whatever reason. The spine is what a borrower sees on the shelf; if he can't read it, he's unlikely to fish it down out of pure curiosity.

NOTE: Just for fun, it's interesting to know that the Spanish Royal library consistently shelved books with the spines to the wall-which, since all the volumes had gilt page-edges, created a magnificent effect--a wall of gold. It also must have given the librarian fits.

SECOND NOTE: Leather-bound books present a special problem, inasmuch as leather which has never been properly renovated tends to dry out and crack along the creases beside the spine. In Chapter Fourteen we shall deal with this problem. Forget it for the moment.

Before we go on, let's face it--a sizable body of librarians dislike "backed" books. They prefer to bind. Rebound books look more uniform on the shelves. The stamped-in gilt lettering matches all along the shelf. The grained or pebbled buckram lasts indefinitely. Whereas "backed" books have a--well, a home-made look about them, largely because of the individual lettering. The best of markers can't approach a stamping machine.

But since we are agreed that re-binding is a horrific expense, let's consider what's to be said for "backing" books.

In the first place, and most important, a properly "backed" book nowadays can be almost as sturdy as a re-bound one, and much easier to read. That is, it will open flat and stay open without a couple of guardian hands clutching the pages. This permits the reader to put polish on her nails, do up her hair, or even knit. (People do knit and read at the same time. I do myself. There's no limit to the peculiarities of people who read books.) The male reader is able to lay a do-it-yourself book open on his work-bench while he follows instructions. This is largely impossible with a "re-bound" book.

Second, if the new spine is properly put on, and the book-cloth employed is good-looking, the average borrower simply doesn't know the difference. He reaches first, naturally, for a book looking shiny and new in a plastic cover protecting the dust-jacket, even if it happens to be a new edition of "Moby Dick." After that, he plays no favorites between "re-bound" books and "backed" books because he doesn't know that there is any difference, and cares less. Provided that the new back is put on in a professional manner, and the marking is reasonably neat, it should make no difference at all to circulation whether you bind or back. Let your budget be your guide.

Coming down from theory to practice, we arrive at the singularly complex problem of describing in words -- with an assist from the illustrator -- how to put a new back on a book. The job itself is not at all difficult. It

Why, When and How to Replace a Spine

requires care, and some practice to do a really handsome example, but in itself it isn't nearly as difficult as most handicrafts. May I ask you--pretty please--to read what follows twice? The first time it may seem a trifle complicated, but I promise that the second time around it will smooth out like magic. And after you've actually put on a back, you'll wonder why you ever thought it a problem at all.

First of all, make all other necessary repairs to the book. Putting on a new back comes last.

Now, tear off the damaged spine and throw it away. (There is a school of thought which believes in keeping the title, if it is still legible, and attaching it to the new spine. You may do so if you wish. I doubt if you'll really like the result. It has a patchy effect. None the less, it's probably a good idea if you have no one around who can print decently, and the plastic adhesive will hold the title in place quite securely, which was never the case with plain glue or paste.)

With your knife, or an Exacto-knife if you have one, cut away a half-inch of the cover-cloth on either side of the spine. (Fig. 16). Use a ruler to get a sharp, clean line.

Figure 16

NOTE: If the front cover-cloth has a design, or a fancy title, or any sort of decoration, use your artistic discrimination as to how much of the cover-cloth to cut away. You want the finished book to look as much like the original as possible. You can cut away as little as a quarter of an inch or as much as two inches; half an inch is recommended for plain, undecorated covers. In the case of older books bound under the influence of William Morris, it is often the case that the spine was originally covered with cover-cloth of a contrasting color to the rest of the book. In such a case, remove the whole spine-cover.

Next, working with great care and using your blunt-pointed knife, lift up another half inch of the cover-cloth. (Fig. 17). Slit it top and bottom, but be careful not to tear or cut it anywhere else. (Paper-covered books will be considered later.)

The next step is protective and forward-looking. Unless you have already had occasion to do so, in putting in a hinge, scrape away from the backs of the signatures whatever dried glue and tired "super" will come loose without too vigorous treatment. Any time you can get at the backs of the signatures of a book, for any purpose, this preventive medicine is in order. Cover the backs-of-the-signatures with a good coat of **HEAVY DILUTION**, allow to dry, and wax freely.

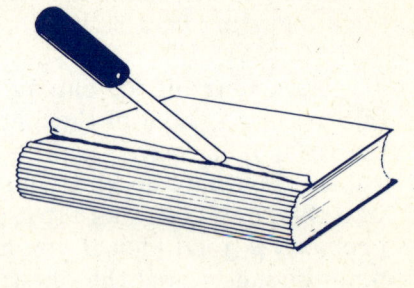

Figure 17

While the backs-of-the-signatures are drying, we will prepare the new back.

Take a strip of new book-cloth and a strip of brown paper from your box of supplies. Trim the strip of brown paper to the exact width of the backs-of-the-signatures, and to the exact length of the side-covers.

This is vitally important.

The brown paper must be exactly the width of the backs-of-the-signatures--<u>not</u> the width between the edges

Why, When and How to Replace a Spine

of the side-covers, but the precise distance between the ledge at front and back of the contents, taking into consideration the small but definite curve of the contents. It must be exactly the length of the side-covers, and not the length of the contents. These measurements may vary only by an eighth of an inch, but you must be accurate about them. The trimming of this strip of brown paper is the secret of a professional-looking back.

Very good.

Take the strip of book-cloth and trim it to a length exactly two inches longer than the strip of brown paper. Then measure it to fit well under the lifted cover-cloth on either side of the spine. The fit should be close but easy. You don't want it skin-tight, because the new spine must accommodate the curve of the backs-of-the-signatures and also give perhaps an eighth of an inch tolerance for the creases along either side of the spine. Fortunately, since you have a half-inch or so of space on either side, this measurement is not very critical. Just don't be skimpy. You want the original cover-cloth to come down over the new book-cloth for at least a quarter of an inch; a half-inch will be better.

Lay the strip of book-cloth down with the wrong side uppermost. In the exact center, attach the strip of brown paper with **LIGHT DILUTION.** (Fig. 18). (If you are using gummed paper, lay the stickum-ed side on the cloth.)

Cut in from each of the four corners of the book-cloth strip to each of the four corners of the brown paper. If you haven't a steady hand and a good eye, use a ruler and red pencil to make guide lines.

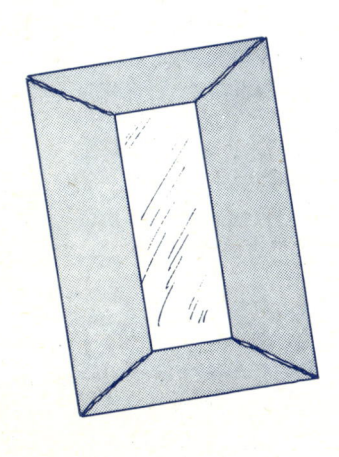

Figure 18

This gives you a wedge-shaped flap top and bottom. Fold these flaps over and attach them with LIGHT DILUTION. (Fig. 19).

NOTE: In some cases, notably with very narrow books, you may find that these wedge-shaped flaps when folded down extend on either side past the edge of the book-cloth strip. Simply trim the flaps back even with the edge of the cloth.

If you feel inclined to be fancy, you may now clip off the points of the four peaks left at the corners of the book-cloth strip, so as to make neat square ends.

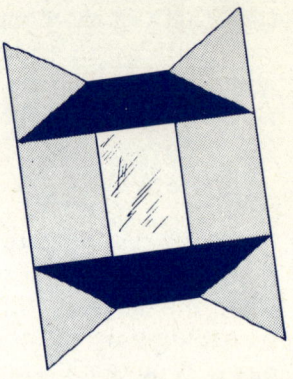

Figure 19

It is now time to put the book and the new back together. Presumably by now the backs-of-the-signatures are thoroughly dry and carefully waxed. If not, you'll have to wait. And this illustrates the advantages of using an assembly-line technique on backing. It is efficient to prepare a number of books for backing, set them aside to dry, and prepare the backs for them at one fell swoop. Then, without loss of time, the new backs are put on the prepared books and the whole job finished off at once.

Paint the wrong side of the book-cloth strip with HEAVY DILUTION. You will not, of course, paint the brown paper strip, and you will equally of course not touch the portions of the flaps which cover brown paper at top and bottom. (See Fig. 19 again).

Lay the backs-of-the-signatures carefully upon the brown paper strip, centering precisely, and smooth the new book-cloth gently up onto the side-covers.

Why, When and How to Replace a Spine

Turn the book onto one side, with the spine towards you, and use the bone to smooth the new book-cloth down firmly onto the side-board and press out any excess plastic adhesive which might otherwise create bubbles or buckles in the cloth.   Reverse the book and do the same for the other side.

Next, run the bone firmly down the edge of the spine on either side, just where the spine meets the side-covers, to create the necessary crease or groove which was there originally. (Fig. 20).

Now, coat the half-inch or so of new book-cloth which will be under the lifted sections of the original cover-cloth with HEAVY DILUTION, and smooth the lifted portions down into place. Use the bone again to force any excess plastic adhesive out from under the cover-cloth, and wipe whatever oozes out away with a damp cloth.

Figure 20

Turn the four points or peaks of the new back over onto the inside of the side-covers and attach them with HEAVY DILUTION. (Fig.21). Slip sheets of waxed paper between side-covers and contents, close the book, and wipe off any plastic adhesive which may have got smeared on the book as you were working. Once more use the edge of the bone to make the creases sharp and distinct.

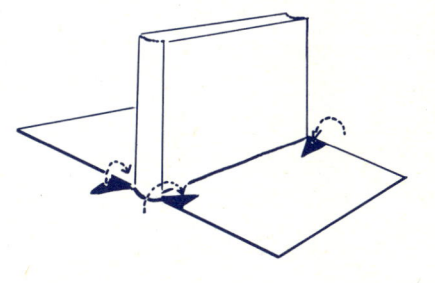

That's it.

Figure 21

There you have a newly-backed book to be proud of. Let it dry over-night--you're working now with heavier materials than hinges--and it's ready to be marked and sent back to the wars.

It's not nearly as complicated as it sounds. Remember, you promised to go back and re-read the directions? All right, go back and do so.

Well, wasn't I right? It's easy, really.

NOTE: You can, if you wish, dispense with lifting the original cover-cloth. You can put the new book-cloth over it instead. It doesn't make quite so sharp a job, but it saves a small amount of time. It is even imperative when you are dealing with a paper-covered book-- by which I mean a book whose hard side covers are sheathed in paper instead of cloth. Mostly you can't get the paper up without tearing it, so the new book-cloth must go down on top instead of underneath.

NOTE AGAIN: We haven't said anything about the choice of colors in book-cloth for new backs. Book-cloth comes in a rainbow of colors, but unless you can afford to keep a whale of a lot of stuff on hand, you'll probably find it practical to select a few colors and stick to them. Navy blue goes with practically any color, and isn't as depressing as black. A good hunter's green is also useful. Pastel shades tend to get dirty and show wear rather quickly. But for morale purposes, and to liven up the shelves, I recommend adding some fire-wagon red. These three basic colors will go with any book in the collection, and sufficiently diversify the shelves, besides allowing the mender some artistic license in her choice. Sets, of course, should be backed in the same color, but there's no law that says duplicate copies have to match; it's even an advantage if they don't.

Chapter Ten
MASTERPIECES

or

Re-Casing, Which the Experts Say Can't Be Done

It happens, puppies being what they are, not to mention small children and other pets, that sometimes a book needs not just a new spine but a whole new casing. This is by no means a hopeless catastrophe.

In fact, it's a delightful challenge.

And it often happens to quite a new book. In the case of a popular novel, it'll be well worth while to do-it-yourself; by the time the book gets back from the bindery, it's dead; you need it for circulation during its brief hour of publicized glory, and you can re-case it yourself overnight. Here's how.

First, remove the ruined casing entirely--spine, side-covers and all.

Next, do whatever is necessary to recondition the contents. If Fido has gnawed front or back pages, remove them, re-type the material, and attach the typed pages to the contents with heavy dilution. Use regular twenty-pound bond, cut to fit and in the case of title pages, typed in as close a reproduction of the original as possible.

If Fido has also gnawed along the edges of the pages, creating a ragged effect, trim the page-edges down evenly as far as necessary. It may very well be that while munching, Fido has caused the cover-cloth to bleed and stain the edges of the pages pink or blue or green. Don't let that dismay you. When you have finished casing the book, as hereinafter directed, simply put it into the press under maximum pressure, or weight it heavily with several large books, and paint the edges of the pages with poster-paint slightly darker than the stain. Many books are so tinted along the page edges by the publisher, so nobody will think oddly of it, and Fido's damage will be quite invisible.

Now to create a brand-new casing.

For this we must be prepared.

Obviously, you discard some books, in spite of your phenomenal success in mending. Otherwise the stacks would split at the seams. So, when you do, examine the discards carefully and remove, with a sharp knife, all the side-covers which are still in pretty good shape. Put them aside, and try to assemble a varied assortment, in as many different sizes and shapes as possible.

From this collection you now select a pair of side-covers which fit the book on which you are working. If no pair fits exactly, use the paper-cutter to trim down a pair to the right size--remembering that side-covers should always jut out about an eighth of an inch beyond the edge of the contents.

Attach these side-covers to the contents precisely as directed in Chapter Seven.

Re-Casing, Which the Experts Say Can't Be Done

If these new covers (new to this particular book, that is) are in good condition and of a suitable color, and haven't had to be trimmed, you may then simply put on a new back and there you are.

Otherwise, we must perform the most complicated operation in all mending, and one which, when successful, you carry around with you and display to all and sundry, purring with disgusting pride.

Don't tackle it until you've mastered backing technique. It's only an extension of the simple backing routine, and when you have that down pat, you can go on to re-casing with perfect confidence.

You'll need, first, a strip of brown paper measured and trimmed exactly as for a back.

Second, you'll need a piece of book-cloth large enough to cover the entire book, plus a good quarter-inch to lap over the inside of each side cover, plus another quarter-inch or so for the creases.

To make this measurement, open the book--meaning the contents which has been fastened into the new covers--down the center, so that the side-covers lie flat against the book-cloth. Measure three-quarters of an inch beyond the side covers on either side, and for the other measurement, add two inches to the length of the side-covers.

This is perhaps a shade generous, but it's easier to trim than to stretch. The rondure of the signatures, the depth of the creases--these make a small but perceptible difference. It's better to have a little more cloth than you need. With practice, you'll be able to judge easily just about how to trim for any given book.

Find the exact center of this piece of book-cloth, laying it down as an oblong with the with the wrong side up, and mark this center point. Measure an inch on either side of this mark, and make two more marks. Do this top and bottom. Next, center the strip of brown paper exactly in the middle of the oblong and attach with LIGHT DILUTION. (Fig. 22).

Now, from the four marked points on either side of the center-point, cut in to each of the four corners of the brown paper strip. (Fig. 23). Fold down the wedge-shaped flaps and attach them with LIGHT DILUTION.

NOTE: In the case of a very wide or very narrow book, the inch measurements suggested above may not be serviceable. That is, if the book is more than two inches wide, you'll need somewhat wider flaps. The adjustment is simple, since you know how to put on a back and therefore know what you're aiming at.

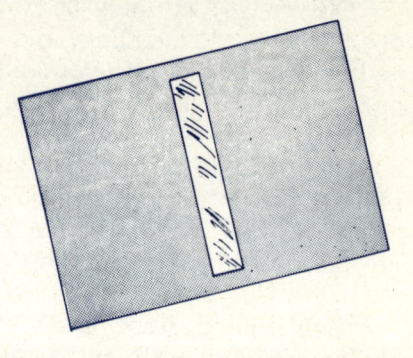

Figure 22

Now, with a ruler, measure three-eighths of an inch up from the fold of the upper wedge-shaped flap and draw a line across the rest of the book-cloth at that point. Cut along this line. (See Fig. 23 again). Do the same at the bottom. You now have a neat new casing all ready to put on.

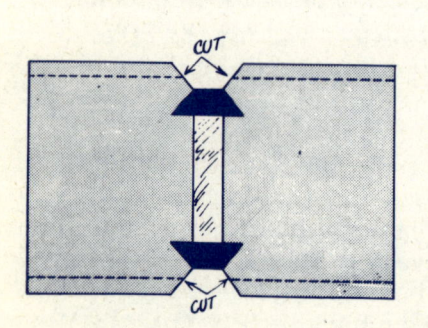

Figure 23

Paint one side-cover, or, if you prefer, the inner surface of one side of the new book-cloth, with LIGHT DILUTION and smooth the new book-cloth into place, being careful to see that the

Re-Casing, Which the Experts Say Can't Be Done

backs of the signatures are centered precisely on the brown paper strip. Fold over the edges of the book cloth and attach to the inside of the side-covers all around the three sides. Either mitre the corners or slit the book-cloth in as far as the edge of the side-cover, whichever makes the neatest corner--this will depend on the heaviness of the book-cloth you are using. Then take the edge of the bone and press it firmly down beside the spine at the edge of the side-cover until you have made a good, distinct crease.

Turn the book over and repeat the operation on the other side-cover.

Lay sheets of waxed paper inside front and back covers and put the book to press overnight.

Once you've done this operation one time, and seen the surprisingly professional-looking result, you'll be tempted to operate on every depressed-looking book in the collection. This is the job which really impresses your colleagues; they may be just polite about your other miracles, but re-casing bugs their eyes out with honest awe.

The icing on the cake consists of finishing up the job with a new set of end-papers. If you intend to do this, remember to remove the original end-papers before you put in new hinges.

#1 drawing paper makes a quite satisfactory end-paper, but in a pinch regular typewriter bond can be used.

Before you start, get a nice new book and look to see how end-papers are put in. You observe that they cover the whole of the inside of the side-cover, extending not quite to the very edge on three sides, and that they are fastened down over the ledge of the contents, being pushed firmly into the junction-point where side-cover and contents meet. The rest of the paper simply flaps free, forming a front or back page.

A moment's thought will tell us that if we simply cut an oblong of paper of the proper size to fit the book, we will find ourselves with a minor discrepancy. That is, the paper must be a little smaller than the side-cover, but exactly the same size as the contents. So we will trim one-half of the paper a very little smaller than the other half, and this smaller section will go onto the inside of the side cover. To demonstrate, lay a piece of paper of approximate size in place and with the edge of your bone crease it down onto the ledge where it will properly go. Then trim one side neatly to fit the inside of the side cover. This done, remove the paper, paint the inside of the side-cover, the hinge and the ledge with **LIGHT DILUTION**, and put the end-paper in place, smoothing diligently with a bit of crumpled waxed paper and then with the flat edge of the bone. Be sure to use the bone vigorously to be certain that the new end-paper sticks firmly to the ledge.

Repeat with the other end-paper, put the book to press over night, and behold, your masterpiece is complete.

Apart from the satisfaction which arises from this operation, it's highly useful. It doesn't take half as long as you might expect from reading about it; actually, once you've done it a couple of times, it takes only a few minutes more than a straight backing job. And by means of it you can easily salvage a brand new book which would otherwise have to be replaced, or--better still--renovate an o.p. treasure to meet another fifty years or so of discriminating readership. It's specially useful for unbindable books like Modern Library giants which tend to get dreadfully dingy. It's also valuable in the case of a paper-covered book which you consider worth preserving; with this technique you can easily turn it into a nice-looking hard-cover job which will last indefinitely. Altogether, it's a technique which every mender should take a little time to practice; it will pay dividends.

Chapter Eleven
PREVENTIVE MEDICINE
or
An Apple for the Teacher-Librarian

This is for School Librarians.

It may also be of interest to librarians in small branches, especially those with a large juvenile collection, and to Bookmobile librarians.

But primarily it's for you, dear teacher-librarian. You have--as if I needed to remind you--special problems.

They include the complete absence of time to mend, not to mention lack of space, both for working and for storing materials. There is also a notable lack of money for bindery or replacement.

About the only thing you don't lack is books to be mended.

Obviously, what you need is a stream-lined technique which will preserve the collection speedily and yet effectively, since it's no great gain to mend a book quickly if you have to do it all over again in a week or two. This technique should be simple enough to be taught to student-helpers, and rapid enough to be practiced by your own harried hands in the absence of any help at all.

O.K. Here you are.

You will need plastic adhesive--an eight-ounce bottle is the most practical purchase. Two brushes, one small, one larger, as described in Chapter Three. A roll of permanent mending tape, with scissors or--better--a dispenser-holder. Two small jars--cosmetic jars or the like, as were described in Chapter Three. A box of waxed paper. A clean cloth of some sort--cheesecloth or any light dust-cloth will do. And some old newspapers to work on.

That's all, and the whole business takes up practically no storage space. As for working space, just shove your desk blotter aside, or put it on the floor, and spread the newspaper in its place.

With this equipment you aren't going to make extensive repairs. What you are going to do is practice a kind of preventive medicine. Temporarily abandoning to their fate those books which need the repairs which will be discussed in the next chapter--the beat-up juveniles, that is--you are going to concentrate upon those books which are still fairly new and reasonably intact. (Whenever you have time, you can consult the next chapter and renovate the horribles to your heart's content.) Meantime, your object is to cut down the production of stretcher-cases, and what I am about to recommend is unconditionally guaranteed to achieve this end with the minimum of effort.

Your only preparation consists in making a suitable dilution. This is simply done. Half-fill one of your two small cosmetic or poster-paint jars with plastic adhesive and add enough water to bring the level of the dilution to the three-quarters-full point. Fill the other jar with water, in which to leave the brushes while they aren't in use. Keep the piece of cloth handy, to use in drying the brushes before dipping them into the plastic adhesive.

> NOTE: At this point you are asking, "Why make a dilution at all? Why not just dip into the original jar?" There are several reasons why not, and they are as follows:
> First, unless you choose a plastic adhesive of a very low viscosity--that is, one into which the manufacturer has introduced quite a lot of water--you will find that working with the original is slow and rather difficult. The brush drags on the paper and you have to keep dipping and dipping again.
> Second, you use a lot more plastic adhesive than you need, which is definitely not economical.
> Third, inevitably a certain amount of dirt and discoloration is transferred from the books to the plastic adhesive by means of the brushes, so that by the time the container is half-empty the contents assumes a brownish and unappetizing look.
> But by taking the very small amount of time and trouble required to mix a small amount of dilution, you secure much greater ease and efficiency, and your original container, being promptly capped and put away, is protected from evaporation and from dirt and you get full use of every drop.

At this point we must elaborate a little.

If you catch a book at the very first sign of collapse and fix it--immediately--you will find that mending becomes a great deal less of a problem. Even more than with an adult collection does prompt and informed care pay off with juveniles. This is partly psychological. Most children are reasonably respectful of a book in good condition, but the minute it becomes obvious to them that the library doesn't care what sort of shape the book is in, they take their cue and make matters worse. You are obviously in a quite untenable moral position when you rebuke a kid for tearing a page when he knows, and you know, that half the books on the shelves have torn pages. The sprouts are terribly logical about things like that.

So in your desk drawer should live a roll of permanent mending tape, preferably in a dispenser, and come into action with the first small tear in a page. If you wait for the tear to get bigger, bigger is what it will get on the very next circulation. Nothing is simpler than slapping tape on a tear, and if you can train yourself or your assistant to make this procedure automatic and habitual, you will right there get a head start on the mending problem. You may want to keep a bottle of crayon-remover along with the tape.

What mending, then, are we going to do in this precious half-hour or so which we have wangled for the purpose?

We are going to confine ourselves to three very simple procedures. Any book which requires more extensive repair will have to wait.

The first and simplest of all is described back in Chapter Six. It consists of dipping the HANDLE of the small brush into the plastic adhesive and running the handle down the inside of the spine at either hinge. This repair should be made the instant the need for it becomes apparent. Simply hold the book up by the side-boards; if the contents flaps forward, free from the spine, it's time to fix it. (See illustration in Chapter Six.) Stacks and stacks of such books can be repaired in half an hour; it's the quickest and easiest repair of all; and yet, if it is faithfully done as soon as the book needs it, it will so reinforce the contents that the need for major repairs will be postponed for months and months.

The second procedure is also detailed carefully in Chapter Six, and consists of replacing the end-papers when they have loosened themselves from the "ledge." (See Chapter Six for illustration and complete instructions.) This repair takes less than a minute, and in no way impairs the book for subsequent rebinding; it just puts off that evil day for a delightfully long period.

The third quick repair is to spines which have torn at top or bottom, or begun to split along the hinges where the side-cover meets the outside of the spine. Using the larger brush, simply swab the spine with plastic adhesive and use your fingers to fit the worn or torn sections together as soon as the dilution becomes sufficiently tacky to hold--a few minutes will usually do it, having regard to the weather as has been explained. When dry, the plastic adhesive makes quite a solid seal which small fingers will have trouble prying loose. If you wish to give the spine a further coat of lacquer or shellac, there's no law against it, but it isn't absolutely essential.

> WARNING: This quite infallible method of keeping juveniles painlessly in repair will work ONLY if it is strictly adhered to. You must resist the temptation to let a book go out "just one more time" as sternly as a reducer avoids a candy bar. This is not going to be easy, because at first it's going to seem that you are wasting precious time on books which, compared to the rest of the collection, are really in pretty fair shape. And this is true. The point is that by expending this time on comparatively new books, you keep them that way. Thus the production of horribles is halted. Naturally, every so often, a book will meet disaster in some major form, but by following strictly

this "stitch in time" formula the slow, inevitable deterioration of a new book into a mess is checked at the very outset.

In the next chapter we shall consider how to mend books which have got past this "catch-'em-alive-o" stage. What I am guaranteeing here is that if you follow this routine for a year--just one year--you will find that the number of ragged objects piled in a closet waiting for detailed attention has shrunk miraculously. If, in the course of that year, you have managed to set aside a few hours here and there to practice the techniques advocated in the next chapter, there may not be any pile at all. Certainly by the end of the next year, mending will have ceased to be a major headache.

NOTE: Not that I wish to be quoted as regarding mending as a headache. Not me! But I admit there are several schools of thought on the subject.

Chapter Twelve
THE LOWER DEPTHS
or
Juvenile Delinquents

We now enter the world of the purely gruesome.

To wit, juveniles.

The scheme I have elaborated in the preceding chapter will do much to keep even juveniles in good shape for longer than you now believe possible, but there will come a time. The darling little fiends are twice as ingenious as book-makers, book-binders or book-fixers; they represent the original Irresistible Force. (This is no place for criticism, but in some cases it almost looks as if the children are simply expressing their intelligent distaste for the reading matter. We won't go into that.) Anyway, in due time juveniles must be mended thoroughly.

Of the making of juvenile books there is no end, and some of the methods adopted to make the books last through at least a few circulations are distinctly clever. Trouble is, the more solidly constructed they are to start with, the harder it is to repair them when once the kids have solved the problem--as they inevitably and cheerfully do. Notably the heavily-stapled readers and the pre-bound books with the handsome, slickly shiny covers. It is possible to repair them, but it isn't easy, and the question arises whether the time involved is worth it. Circumstances must be allowed to alter cases, here as everywhere else.

Obviously, quite a lot of books for children are constructed, and therefore repaired, in precisely the same fashion as adult books; these present no problem. Trouble pokes its head up when we are faced with readers, jjs, picture books and the like. These frayed and dingy objects, in the average collection, are enough to discourage anyone. Some libraries put pathetic little printed notices inside the covers, urging the youngsters to wash their hands before reading. It would often be more to the point, considering the state of some of the books, to urge the poor little bookworms to wash their hands after_wards._

Courage! It's not hopeless, after all. Brave souls have penetrated this desolate territory and come back, weary but triumphant, with techniques which work quite well and don't take too much time. (And if any intrepid innovators exist whom I haven't been able to discover, a word from them would be deeply appreciated.)

Picture-books--the thin, usually over-sized kind which consist of two or perhaps three skinny signatures-- are quite easily repaired.

Remove the contents altogether (unless this has already been accomplished by the cherubs) from the casing. Trim the frayed end-papers neatly back to the edges of the side-covers. Gently scrape any dried glue from the backs-of-the-signatures.

Put the signatures, carefully aligned with each other, into a press or under a weight, so that the backs-of-the-signatures project about half an inch. Coat the backs-of-the-signatures and a quarter of an inch of the first and last pages with HEAVY DILUTION. Allow to dry.

Now. Cut a piece of stitched hinge-tape the length of

the contents. Apply a coat of **LIGHT DILUTION** to the backs of the signatures and a half-inch of the first and last page. Separate two flaps of the hinge-tape and attach these flaps over the backs of the signatures and up over the first and last pages, shaping carefully so that the line of stitching runs exactly down the middle of the backs-of-the-signatures. (Fig. 24). Allow to dry.

Then attach the other two flaps to the inside of the side-covers, using **LIGHT DILUTION**. When dry, wax all hinge surfaces freely.

Figure 24

You will very likely find, when this operation is finished, that the contents now protrudes slightly--perhaps an eighth of an inch--beyond the edges of the side-covers. This is because in the original casing the contents fitted slightly further back into the spine. Such narrow spines are not curved, but box-shaped, and there may sometimes be as much as three-eighths of an inch of space between the squared back of the spine and the backs-of-the-signatures. The reason that it is not recommended to adjust the new hinges so that the contents takes its original position is first, that it ain't easy to do so, and second, you may very well want to put on a new back some time, and you will then find that to have the backs-of-the-signatures level with the side-covers will make the job very much easier. As for the bit of contents that sticks out, this is easily remedied. Just chop it off even with the side-covers. Such books ordinarily have enormous margins and very little text, and a slight "cropping" of the pages will be hardly noticeable. Use scissors or a paper-cutter.

When you do wish to replace the original back, the process is exactly the same as for an adult book, and is described at length in Chapter Nine. I would only add that a little time can be saved by attaching the new book-cloth <u>over</u> the original on the side-covers (and this is of course the only thing you can do when the original casing is covered with thin decorative paper instead of some kind of fabric.) There is no great point in worrying about aesthetics in this case; so long as the new back is neat and brightly-colored, the kids will like it.

> NOTE: But surely a great deal of time can be saved by simply slapping a piece of stickum-ed tape over the original back? Yes, it can indeed. It is quick, and it looks good, too. My only objection is that it isn't awfully durable. Not, mind you, that the tape won't wear. It's that it won't get a chance to. Little fingers quickly discover that you can pry the tape loose along the edges, and if you think that little fingers will resist so doing, you belong in a Rare Books Room. It takes only a little longer to put on a genuine back, and while I'd be the last to guarantee that this will altogether foil the eager little digits, it'll give them a dickens of a lot harder time.
>
> But if you want to use the stickum-ed tape, which after all does come in a nice convenient roll and is frequently handsome to look at, you can easily ignore the stickum and use LIGHT DILUTION just as if you were dealing with plain cloth. This is quite durable, even if slightly extravagant.

If you have conscientiously repaired each tear as it appeared, you will find not nearly so many lopped and truncated pages as you expect, but there are bound to be some. These can be dealt with in three fashions.

- If all the pieces of the page survive, put them together with the permanent mending tape.
- If a jagged hunk has disappeared entirely, cut and shape a piece of typewriter bond to fit and fill out

Juvenile Delinquents 85

> the page and attach it by a narrow line of HEAVY DILUTION to the remaining section. (This at least creates the impression that a torn page is BAD.)
> - If the book is of sufficient value to justify the effort, remove the whole damaged page and type the material onto a sheet of typewriter bond cut to match the contents. This new page can then be tipped in as indicated in Chapter Seven.

NOTE: This matter of torn pages really requires a special chapter on parent-librarian relations. Instead of the printed notice about hand-washing, juveniles ought to carry a large red notice saying, "PLEASE don't repair torn pages with ordinary transparent tape!" But you know what would happen then. All those helpful, virtuously apologetic parents would fix the page somehow--probably with masking tape or sticking plaster or maybe Dad's black friction tape. No wonder the juvenile mending department honestly, if deplorably, prefers the bare-faced parent who insists that "the book was like that when Johnnie got it!"

Now for some real fancy stuff.

Stapled-type readers sometimes lose a cover long before the contents is ready for discard. (Fig.25). The cover can be replaced. It's something of a process, but it works.

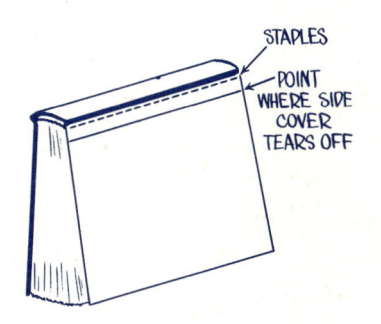

Figure 25

Cut a strip of stitched hinge-tape the length of the contents. Open out two flaps, and line the stitching up with the point where the side-cover came loose (this is usually about half an inch from the back of the spine.) Attach the top flap to the side of the spine which covers the staples, and the bottom flap to the first page of the contents, using LIGHT DILUTION. Allow to dry.

Now insert the side-cover between the two remaining flaps. Use LIGHT DILUTION to attach one flap to the inside of the side-cover and the other to the outside. In doing so, make sure that the inside flap lies flat at the stitching, while the outer flap is fitted over the edge of the side-cover. Thus, the newly-attached cover will open easily and close flat against the contents. Insert waxed paper under the side-cover and allow to dry.

At this point we have salvaged the book, but it doesn't look like much. Obviously we must cover the hinge-flaps which appear outside the covers, and for this we construct a new back just as in Chapter Nine, but we OMIT the brown paper. Cut the wedge-shaped flaps wide enough so that when folded down, the fold will reach the point where the side-covers are attached to the contents. Cover the entire surface of this new back, on the wrong side, with LIGHT DILUTION and put it on. (In this case, you want the new back to adhere firmly to the whole spine and to extend far enough over the side-covers to hide the hinge-flap.) Smooth down firmly all over and allow to dry. The result is quite solid and durable, and looks much the same as the original casing.

This is one place where the stickum-ed tape, put on with LIGHT DILUTION, works very well and saves considerable time. Therefore, by all means use it.

Nothing that I've encountered yet will stick permanently to the highly-glazed side-covers of pre-bound books, unless you use a solvent to destroy the glaze-which will obviously ruin the looks of the book. So, when you want to renew a back on such, you had better make it very, very narrow and see that it doesn't lap over onto the glazed part at all. In this case, also, omit brown paper and attach

Juvenile Delinquents

the whole new back solidly to the surface beneath. Or, still more simply, just attach a strip of stickum-ed tape with LIGHT DILUTION to cover the old back.

Juveniles, by their very nature, tend to provide all manner of special, even unique, problems. To detail all the ways in which juveniles can come apart would be tedious and quite useless, since the very next day would bring up something new. The important thing for a mender of juveniles to develop is a flexible ingenuity. Once you realize that repairs <u>can</u> be made, and made to last, you'll find that what used to be a real dead-end street of a job is suddenly quite fascinating. Learning to out-wit the destructive abilities of the sprouts is an entertaining game. You won't win, of course, but you have a challenge to meet, and just giving the little darlings trouble is quite satisfactory. When they're reduced to tearing out parts of pages, you've scored a moral victory.

NOTE: Libraries which possess Bookmobiles also possess very special mending problems. I don't mean just the lack of space and time; presumably a Bookmobile has some sort of home base where such activities take place. The specially difficult aspect arises from the atmospheric conditions in a Bookmobile. It is dealt with here because most Bookmobiles have primarily juvenile collections, but the remarks apply equally to the adult collection.

Thus. The books line up against the sides of the truck, which no matter how well insulated are much hotter in summer sunshine and much colder in a blizzard than any library shelving. When the doors open, in comes a draft of outdoor air--baking hot, driving wet, snow-laden, or whatever. Customers track in mud and water in wet weather, and this creates a heavy humidity. When the electric heaters are turned on, certain sections of shelving are in a direct line with the blast of hot air. If the Bookmobile doesn't rate a heated garage, it parks over nights and weekends in wintertime in bitter temperatures--and in fine summer climates, it may spend hours on an unshaded plaza and become as cozy inside as a slow oven.

Nothing can be done about all this, of course.

But it should be noted that mending the Bookmobile collection requires even greater care and immediacy than any other. Cheap glues and pastes, bargain bookcloth, short-cuts--these are miserably poor economy. Only the very best materials, carefully used, can hope to beat Nature, which in a Bookmobile is seldom mild. A skilled, devoted and pampered mender, provided with a small extra budget of time and money, is as essential to a Bookmobile as a spare tire. It is fortunate that the plastic adhesive is well adapted to sudden changes in temperature and humidity, but it will also be wise for the personnel to provide themselves with a chunk of the water-proofing wax, with which to vigorously scrub hinges which show signs of sticking, since the original application may wear off under the stress of frequently altering atmosphere. This extra precaution, plus a particularly eagle eye for needed repairs, will go far to keep a Bookmobile collection in good shape in spite of the special hazards to which it is subjected.

Chapter Thirteen
MIRACLE IN THE STACKS
or
In Re: Reference Departments

Reference Librarians, my distinguished colleagues, may I invite your attention? If you haven't heard, the plastic adhesive is your special and stupendous miracle. It's for you, believe me.

Naturally you have books--usually rather more ancient and battered than those in circulating collections, though the mouse's tooth of time has done most of the damage--and you'll find the mending techniques heretofore described useful, plus the chapter to come on the preservation of leather bindings. At this point I'm thinking of periodicals. Those miserable things. Those problem children.

Any library worth its salt, believing that to subscribe to the Reader's Guide is a waste of excellent money unless it also has a fair representation of the magazines therein listed, devotes a large section of stack space to magazines. I can describe that stack with my eyes shut-- which is rather a good way to keep them. There are the serried ranks of handsomely bound periodicals, looking quite as expensive as they are. Gold titles, heavy side- covers warranted not to warp, heavy simulated leather. Beautiful. Unhappily, each series runs out somewhere in the thirties, except in a few limited cases. You remember the thirties? That was when budgets suffered a terrible shrinking, and almost at the same time, up popped a slew of new and useful magazines which often continue to flourish to this very day. Since then, bindery costs have risen steadily, along with everything else, and the problem of which magazines to bind year in and year out, and how long to store those which can't possibly be fitted into the binding budget, has become a major headache.

The compromise, the universal compromise, has been to tie up bundles of unbound magazines and pile them on shelves. Have I any need to describe the result? Dust collects on these untidy, rope-bound bundles. When someone asks for a given issue, you unpile all the bundles above that year, untie the required bundle, remove the issue, and take time out to cough yourself silly in the clouds of dust. Then you wipe off the selected magazine, pile the rest of the bundles back onto the shelf so that you can clamber out of the stack aisle, and resolve to go into some other line of work at the earliest opportunity.

Aha! The hour of liberation has struck.

You'll need a brush--the larger of the two brushes described in Chapter Three will do nicely. A bottle of the plastic adhesive. A small jar (as usual, a cosmetic or poster-paint jar) which you will half-fill with plastic adhesive, adding to it exactly two teaspoonful of water (assuming that you are using a brand which is close to 1400 cps viscosity; lighter dilutions may have to be used just as they come from the bottle.) If you can manage it, a book-press is decidedly useful. But not essential; you can do without it.

Take a year's issue of any given magazine. If the pile measures more than two-and-a-half inches in height, divide the issues into six-month groups. If it measures

In Re Reference Departments

less, be thankful. Weight, with the backs sticking out over a shelf or table, or insert in the press. You'll note that what you now have resembles very closely a group of signatures, and we shall so treat them.

Paint the whole surface of the backs-of-the-magazines with plastic adhesive, being lavish and lapping over about a quarter-inch onto the first page of the top magazine and the last page of the bottom one. (Fig. 26). Allow to dry thoroughly. Give it another and equally lavish coat. While this is drying, type up neat labels giving the title, dates, and any other useful information--volume number and the like--and when the surface is quite dry, attach these labels with the plastic adhesive. Rub the whole surface with wax.

Figure 26

The resulting "book" can easily be stored upright on a shelf, except that it may require book-ends. It's quite astonishing how much usage these home-made volumes can take, but if an unusually active researcher manages to detach a single issue, or even split the group in two--this hardly ever happens unless he drops it from a considerable height--just give the backs another coat of plastic adhesive and make new labels.

If you wish, and have the time and money, there is nothing to prevent you using cardboard magazine binders, similar to but much larger than pamphlet binders, which are carried by most of the supply houses, to encase these collected magazines. Use the plastic adhesive first, to create a firm volume, and then insert into the binder, using **LIGHT DILUTION** to reinforce the stickum with which the binder-hinges are anointed. Or you can create your own binders, using any old book-covers which happen to fit or sheets of heavy press-board; the procedure is precisely the same as that described in Chapter Nine. Both procedures enhance the looks of the shelves and naturally give added protection to the magazines. Depends mostly on how much time you have, what you decide to do.

And what, I hear some of you saying with raised eyebrows, about a real casing job--you know, the kind that involves a bookbinder's saw and is for the ages?

Well, yes. If you wish to invest in a book-press-- you'll need it for this--you can do a really lasting job, which will be practically impervious to dropping or even flinging. My own feeling is that in the sacrosanct purlieus of a Reference Room, borrowers are very well behaved and don't put much strain on the magazines they carry to a table, or have carried to them by properly trained pages. But if you make a practice of loaning out bound magazines, this more durable process is definitely in order.

Line up the magazines in the press, apply suitable pressure, and up-end the press so that the backs of the magazines are handily visible. Take a bookbinder's saw (a coping-saw borrowed from the custodian will do almost as well) and make three or four incisions across the backs. (Fig. 27). These incisions are V-shaped and deep enough to reach the center signature of each magazine. Paint the whole surface, and especially the depths of the incisions, with plastic adhesive. Then cut lengths of soft, sturdy cord-- a special cord is sold for the purpose by the supply houses, but if you haven't any on hand, red legal tape or something similar will serve--

Figure 27

In Re Reference Departments 93

and insert a length firmly into each incision. Allow to dry. Cut off the ends of the cords about a quarter-inch from each side of the backs, and apply a second coat of plastic adhesive to the whole surface. This time make sure that you lap over sufficiently onto the first and last pages to secure the ends of the cords firmly.

Naturally, you can go on after this to put the "volume" into a magazine binder, or construct side-covers and a back, or you can label them as is.

But the simple, original process will enable you to save time and money, and keep your stacks looking civilized; it's entirely a matter of judgment on your part how much more time and effort you need put into the project.

NOTE: Not only Reference Librarians, but everybody on the staff has to remember that Time is the most expensive element in any process. Grudging Time when time is necessary is extravagant; so is spending Time when you don't have to. A lot of libraries are still using pretty archaic methods just because nobody has taken the time to experiment with sensible modern short-cuts; on the other hand, doing a slap-dash and temporary job is a sheer waste of the time involved. Industry knows this and large numbers of young men with clip-boards circulate around factories evaluating time against other factors in the interests of efficient operation. Professional fastnesses like libraries are sometimes a little slow to recognize that Time is economic.

Chapter Fourteen
BEAUTY SALON
or
There's Nothing Like Leather

Originally, books were bound. It was quite a process, involving a great deal of hand work, but the results lasted. In fact, the life of a "bound" book was determined almost wholly by the life of the paper employed for the contents; paper does have a definite life-expectancy and will wither and disintegrate eventually even if untouched by human hands. Rag-paper lasts much longer than pulp-wood stock. Many a book printed in the seventeenth century on rag stock and properly bound is sturdier today than yesterday's "cased" pulp-stock novel.

Up until the nineteenth century or so, books were usually covered with leather. That is, the "cover-cloth" which encased the side-boards (which were first made of wood, and later of heavy cardboard) and formed the spine was genuine leather, usually a soft but durable calf or sheepskin but sometimes much more exotic--Morocco or ostrich-skin or indeed almost anything that could be tanned.

Presently it became an economy to cover only the spine and a few adjoining inches of the side-boards with leather; the rest of the side-covers, with the exception of triangular pieces over the top and bottom corners, was covered with marbled paper or decorative cloth. Nineteenth century authors, who tended to turn out volumes the way the waters came down at Lodore, usually arrived at immortality in a "Collected Works" bound after this fashion--though there may be some doubt about whether the "leather" involved ever saw a pasture.

Then somebody invented a "casing" machine; mass production of books set in; and l'll dogies, whatever else their destiny, ceased to have much to do with book-binding. (Some government publications continued to appear in magnificent sheep or calf for quite a while after cloth had taken over the commercial market, but budgets caught up with even these eventually.)

Who, you are asking, cares?

If you are so asking, you're young in the profession. Any library whose collection dates back to before the first World War knows and loathes leather-bound books. They are beautiful; they are valuable and usually quite irreplaceable; and if you lay a hand on them you instantly become coated with a fine, pale-tan dust which clings like foundation-powder and isn't half so becoming. The fate of a librarian taking inventory among these lovely heirlooms is sad. Nothing will do but to send her to the cleaners at the end of the day.

The reason for this is simple. Leather is, you see, a natural product, not an

There's Nothing Like Leather

artifact. It's skin. Skin needs oil to stay soft and pliable. I don't have to labor this point to librarians who likely invest in skin-cream for their own complexions. If similar care had been taken of your leather-bound volumes from the beginning, you'd have no problem.

Now it is obvious that once the oil has dried out of leather, it can't be really replaced--that is, the leather will never again be what it was in its handsome youth. But there is a technique which can be employed to render even the driest, most perished leather soft, pleasant to handle, and perfectly usable even by a borrower in a white sharkskin suit. It is lengthy but neither difficult nor expensive; it makes an admirable summer job.

You must invest in some additional materials--about a buck's worth. (Additional, that is, to the plastic adhesive.)

To wit:

- one can neat's-foot oil (a neat was an Anglo-Saxon ox, and the oil of his foot is available at any sporting-goods store. Ski-ers know all about it. It will darken leather slightly, whatever the label says, but the chances are that the leather has faded in drying so that the new color is nearer the original shade of the binding)
- one jar saddle soap (from the same source)
- one jar neutral leather cream or colorless paste shoe polish (any shoe-shine place, or even the five-and-ten)
- one small synthetic sponge
- two brushes, similar to the larger of the two recommended in Chapter Three

Cut the sponge into inch-square blocks. One chunk will be used with the saddle-soap and another for the leather cream. When they become badly discolored, discard for fresh pieces.

Fill a poster-paint or cosmetic jar three-quarters full of water. Add a teaspoonful of plastic adhesive and stir. This makes a dilution so thin that it's hardly worth calling it a dilution at all; it will be barely milky.

Spread out lots of old newspapers (and get into a smock; this is going to be sort of splashy.) Stand the book to be treated so that both spine and side-covers can be worked on. (Fig. 28). Dipping a brush into the dilution, paint the whole surface of the leather quickly and thoroughly. If bits of leather have stripped back or curled away, put them back into place with your fingers. Be sure that places where the original polished surface has been scraped or has flaked away get a good coating. You'll find that the water in the dilution soaks into the parched leather almost instantly, turning it dark. Think nothing of it. Just make sure that the whole surface is well covered with this very light sizing. The purpose is to protect the fragile dried leather from damage during subsequent operations, without coating it so heavily that the oils won't penetrate.

Figure 28

Wait until the leather has dried. (This won't take very long, but it is a very good idea to make leather-treatment an assembly-line job. Half a dozen books can be worked on in rotation, moving through one step at a time down the line, with a nice gain in efficiency.)

Moisten a piece of sponge in plain water and rub it vigorously on the saddle soap. Wash the leather with a light, sure touch, using not too much water and rinsing the bit of sponge often (a bowl of lukewarm water is handy for this purpose.) Don't rinse or wipe the leather; leave the soap and suds, such as there are, to dry in. If part of

There's Nothing Like Leather

the side-covers are paper or cloth, wipe them clean with a damp cloth.

> NOTE: Sometimes, in the case of very old books which have circulated, you may be astonished to find that this operation reveals that the dull, dim leather binding is actually a handsome piece of tree-calf, whose pattern comes up like magic as the accumulated dirt of years vanishes. This is a nice experience.

The next step, once the leather is dry again, is to paint the leather with neat's-foot oil. Use your second brush, and work quickly to prevent streaking, but be careful, in the case of combination bindings, not to get the oil onto the paper or cloth areas. Be as lavish with the oil as you like; that leather has been thirsty for years.

The drying period at this point will take longer. But if, after an hour or so, there are still shiny patches of unabsorbed oil, wipe them away with a soft cloth. This usually indicates that at some point in its history the book had a label pasted to it, and the residual stick-um keeps the leather from absorbing the oil. A pity, but nothing can be done about it.

Now add to the remaining dilution in your little jar about as much plastic adhesive as you added in the first place--a teaspoonful, not more. (If by chance you used all the dilution up for the first coating, half-fill your jar with water and add a teaspoonful-and-a-half of plastic adhesive.) Coat the leather surface with this dilution. This time it won't dry in quickly, so you must work deftly to avoid streaking and dripping. It will also take longer to dry. Give it ample time, so that it isn't even tacky.

Finally, moisten a piece of sponge in clean water and wring it out as dry as you can. Apply the neutral leather cream or colorless paste polish with this sponge. Allow to dry for five minutes, and polish with a clean soft cloth.

The result is a smooth, pleasant-smelling, absolutely clean book which handles comfortably, looks well, and is no menace to anyone. A bride could cuddle it up to her wedding gown without a qualm. From being a necessary evil it has become a pride-and-joy.

NOTE: Regardless of the temptation, no part of this admittedly rather lengthy process can be safely omitted. Just painting with neat's-foot oil will do no harm, of course, but the unprotected surface will attract and hold dust worse than ever. Using the plastic adhesive as a protective coating, without the addition of the polish, is plain disastrous; the books will weld together on the shelves. Washing, without the preliminary coat of sizing, will probably remove most of the leather surface altogether. So practice patience and do the job right. It's well worth it.

There is another problem which arises with leather-bound books, especially sets. The spines, though in good enough shape themselves, crack bodily away from the side-covers. There is no really satisfactory cure for this, short of backing, but it is possible to make a repair which will hold a spine which has begun to go but still clings by a few shreds of leather.

Simply fill the cracks with plastic adhesive just as it comes from the jar, using a very small brush and making

There's Nothing Like Leather

several applications, so as to build up a solid filling for the crack. This will definitely not take handling to any extent, but it will keep the spine from falling off the book and thus preserve the looks of the set. Cover the crack, when the plastic adhesive has thoroughly set, with a light coat of the neutral leather cream.

>**NOTE:** If you have very valuable leather-bound books, you may prefer to invest in the special variation of the plastic adhesive which is made and sold just for leather. Your mail will doubtless give you the brand name and supplier. This product has several additives which are designed to keep leather soft and pliable, and has, I believe, the blessing of the British Museum and many of our own archives. When you're dealing with the irreplaceable, a slight additional expense is very well justified.

Chapter Fifteen
FANCY TOUCHES
or
Anybody Can Do Anything

Here we'll try to gather up all the special problems which may confront menders from time to time.

RING BINDERS

A sizable number of books turn up these days in ring-binders--either wire or plastic. This type of binding is extremely practical, especially for the type of material which needs to lie open on a work-bench or desk while the reader follows instructions. Unfortunately, it is not especially practical for library circulation. The bindery won't touch it, and the pages detach so easily that they are just a standing invitation to a borrower to remove what he wants--like a house-plan or a TV schematic or a nice set of formulae which it would take him a day to copy. It is never advisable to tempt that slight touch of larceny which lurks in all of us.

Still, a lot of excellent material comes bound in this fashion, and it's a pity to have to pass it up.

And if you consider that the material is worth a little time and trouble, you no longer need do so.

All that is necessary is for there to be an adequate margin at the inner edge of the pages--that is, for there to be half an inch or so of margin between the holes and the printed text.

The procedure is simple. Remove the binder altogether, using wire-clippers (the custodian will probably do this for you if you look sufficiently helpless, but it's not very hard to manage your own self.) Then use paper-cutter or scissors to trim away the holes. (Fig. 29.)

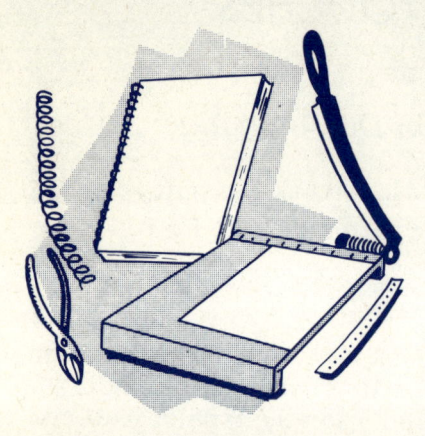

Figure 29

Shape the resulting loose pages into a concave curve, exactly like the pages of a real book (except that there's no way you can create a "ledge") and place in a book-press or under enough weight to hold them firmly. Using **HEAVY DILUTION** and your larger brush, paint them thoroughly. Next, cut a piece of cheesecloth a little wider than, and the same length as, the pile of pages thus fixed together. (Often you can use a piece cut from the waste-cloth you use for drying brushes; it's usually just about the right weight and texture.) Fit this strip carefully over the tacky surface, extending it about a quarter of an inch onto the first and last pages. Fix in place with a coat of **LIGHT DILUTION** and allow to dry thoroughly.

You'll find that this "contents" will open quite comfortably, although it will not, of course, open out flat in quite the way it was originally intended to do. Against this loss you must set the fact that anybody who wants to swipe a page is going to have to cut it out deliberately-- a hardened criminal he!

Anybody Can Do Anything

To finish the job, simply attach the original covers with stitched hinge and supply a new back according to the directions in Chapters Eight and Nine. Or put the contents into a pamphlet binder, attaching the original front cover to the outside of the binder (if you plan to do this, which is probably the simplest procedure, don't shape the pages but leave them squared when you put them together.)

In either case, you have quite a sturdy facsimile of the original book which will take a good deal of wear and tear.

(You can even supply hard-covers from your reserve of used covers, but it isn't altogether a good idea. In the absence of the all-important "ledge" a stiff cover will tend to pull the pages apart eventually.)

LOOSELEAF LEDGERS, ALBUMS, AND SUCH-LIKE

Many libraries possess records--accession lists, financial reports, and the like--which were carefully and laboriously written in spidery long-hand in various types of looseleaf ledger. Time being what it is, these records are probably pretty well along toward disintegration. If you insist on keeping them--most libraries do--they can be treated in the same fashion as the above-discussed ring-binders. It won't be necessary to trim off the holes unless they have already torn away, since nobody is apt to want to tear out a page from these unfascinating antiques.

The same process can be used to give a new lease on life to albums and scrap-books in which clippings have been pasted for reference material.

PHONOGRAPH ALBUMS

The backing process described in Chapter Nine works just as well on a beat-up phonograph album as it does on a book.

For album envelopes which have split along the side

or bottom edge, use plain hinge tape, folded into a trough and attached with LIGHT DILUTION. (Permanent mending tape is not sufficiently strong for the purpose, and brown paper just won't lie flat.)

When an envelope begins to split away from the spine along the fold, reinforce with plain hinge tape and LIGHT DILUTION. If the envelope has become loose altogether, use two strips of plain hinge tape, one under the split and one on top. In all cases, don't forget to wax freely!

ART BOOKS

The makers of expensive art books have a way of inserting their lovely plates in such fashion that the purchaser, if so minded, can easily detach them for framing. Art-loving borrowers shouldn't be asked to wrestle with their consciences in the face of such temptation; on the other hand, smearing the backs of the plates with paste is going to create unlovely bumps and hollows.

The proper procedure is to take the small brush and HEAVY DILUTION. Very delicately run a narrow line of plastic adhesive along the outer edges of the back of each plate. This will attach the plate firmly without disfiguring it. (It takes a steady hand and patience, but when you've paid thirty or forty bucks for a book, it's worth a bit of trouble to make sure that it stays intact.)

OLD NEWSPAPERS

There is a product on the market which invisibly mends tears in newsprint. If you rootle around among the ads you've received you'll doubtless find a supplier. The liquid doesn't work very well on any other kind of stock, but it does work on newsprint, so if you have valuable old newspapers which have suffered extensive tears, or clippings in similar shape, you'll probably find it profitable to invest in a jar. Otherwise, the permanent mending tape is to be preferred to onion-skin, because onion-skin will eventually turn brown and brittle and a second repair will be impossible. (Obviously microfilming is much to be preferred to either process, but alas, for most libraries microfilm is in the dream department.)

RIVER, STAY 'WAY FROM MY DOOR

A leaking pipe in the stacks is a major catastrophe. Even a window left open during a storm means double trouble for the repair squad. Here time is vital; the quicker you work, the better. (It's worth knowing, perhaps, that a leaking steam pipe usually causes damage to books on the upper stack shelves, where the steam can condense on the volumes unseen, whereas a leak in a soil pipe usually confines its ravages to the immediate vicinity.)

Every book which has been exposed to water must be taken off the shelves as soon as possible and allowed to dry--if possible, in the sun. Stand each book upright, with the covers winged out and the pages fanned open. Every so often, as the books dry, flip the pages through to make sure that none of them are stuck together. Sure, the books are going to warp, but never mind that for the moment. The big thing is to get them dry. Even a day's delay can mean mildew.

Once the books are thoroughly dry, it's time to take stock of the damage. If warping is very bad, you'll just have to get a book-press. Remove the contents bodily from the casing, sponge the top and bottom pages rather freely with denatured alcohol, and insert in the press under maximum pressure. Leave for several days. (When the contents comes out, it will smell slightly of vanilla. I have no idea why. It's not unpleasant, and practically vanishes after a week or so.) In some cases, denatured alcohol causes the type or colored plates to run. Test for this first by sponging a section vigorously with alcohol. You <u>can</u> use plain water instead, but the chances are about fifty-fifty that mildew will develop in the pressing. Much depends on the climate at the time. You've certainly nothing to lose by trying, anyway.

It is more than likely that the covers are in much worse condition than the contents, and it will probably be wise to jettison them altogether and re-case the book according to the directions in Chapter Nine, adding a new back to complete the job.

But if warping is slight, the whole book can be pressed with some hope of restoring it to a semblance of its former self. It'll never be the same again, but it may be usable. BUT if the cover, or any part of it, is leather, pressing must be followed immediately by reconditioning according to the directions in Chapter Fourteen--and give it not one but two applications of neat's-foot oil.

Sometimes a book which has become damp develops "bubbles" between the cover-cloth and the side-covers. That is, the cover-cloth rises up in bumps and ridges and looks terrible. If you don't care to go to the bother of putting on a new casing, it is frequently possible to cure this condition.

Take your knife, or the Exacto-knife, and slit the cover-cloth along the top, side and bottom edges of the side-boards. Lift up the cover-cloth from the side-boards and apply HEAVY DILUTION to the exposed surface of the side-boards. Smooth the cover-cloth down into place and put into a book-press under maximum pressure for two days.

And what, you ask unhappily, if you haven't discovered the catastrophe until the books have developed what looks like a flourishing culture of penicillin all over them?

Well, you can always go out and shoot the plumber, or the goon who left the window open.....

When that has been attended to, examine the victims (the books, that is) carefully. If the mildew is mostly on the casings, remove them and throw them away. Re-case the book as heretofore directed. But first you must make sure that you have gotten rid of any mildew spores in the contents. For this, a mild soap and lukewarm water is the best cure. Wash the edges of the pages all around, and also both surfaces of half a dozen of the front and back pages. Use a damp, not wet, cloth. Then place the contents, fanned open, on a sunny windowsill, preferably with the window open if the weather permits, and let it dry thoroughly. The dampened pages will curl up, of course, but once the drying is complete, press as directed above and they ought to come back pretty well to normal. The chances are that soap, sunshine and alcohol will save the day.

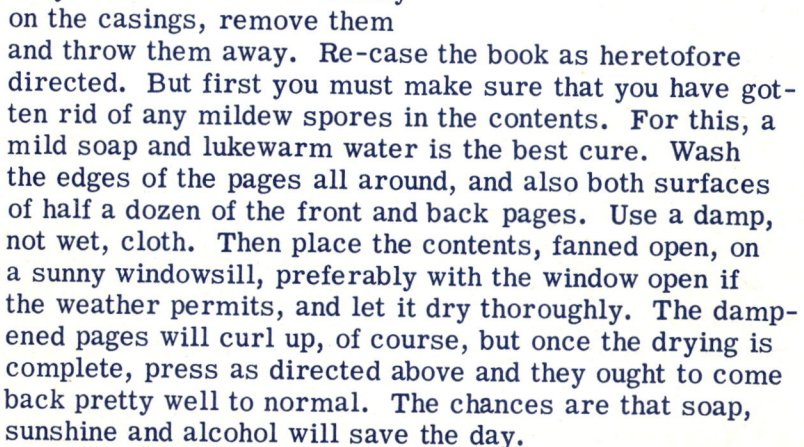

If you feel that you must save the covers, you can try

a desperate remedy. Get some colorless white cider vinegar, or, if your drug-store stocks it, some acetic acid, and sponge the afflicted parts gently after washing with mild soap and water. Then give the book the sun-and-air treatment and a pressing, and pray for the best. It'll likely smell peculiar for a while, and I would counsel you not to shelve it for a week or two, until you're sure that you've effected a cure.

(I have no helpful advice if your crisis occurs in the rainy season. Drying by artificial heat isn't nearly as effective as sunshine. But once again, you've nothing to lose by trying.)

In the perfectly awful case of a stack which is permanently damp, so that for no obvious reason books suddenly turn an unhealthy green, you can try thrusting them under the noses of the trustees, the Building Committee, or whatever is the responsible group, so that eventually they get as sick of them as you are. Meantime, every book should be protected immediately upon acquisition with an extra-heavy coat of book-lacquer or shellac, not just on the spine but all over. And this coating should be renewed just as soon as it shows signs of wearing thin. Leather-bound books should be reconditioned, as directed in Chapter Fourteen, every year (leather makes a dandy culture for mildew, which is as alive and hungry as you or I.) There's really not much else you can do, except to keep an eagle eye out and apply the above-detailed remedies as soon as traces of mildew appear. I bleed for you, and trust that you have Job's patience; you'll need it.

NOTE: These procedures will often save a book which has been dunked in a mud-puddle or a washing-machine by our dear public. It's only worth the trouble, however, if the book is an o.p. of real value.

PAPER-BOUND BOOKS

Quite a lot of valuable material turns up in casings which are simply not intended for library circulation at all. (Actually, no book is so designed, even the most expensive hard-cover job. Books are designed to be bought, read, loaned to Aunt Harriet, and thereafter live peacefully on a bookshelf--yours or Aunt Harriet's, depending upon the skill in book-sneafery of your respected aunt. They are not intended for the rough-and-tumble of library circulation, and there's no use our blaming the publishers. It's up to us to make them serviceable.) I am not here considering the pocket-sized paper-bound reprints; these we will work on in the next chapter. Nor am I thinking immediately of music scores; they'll get a section to themselves right after this.

So what am I thinking of? Of civil service study-books, income-tax manuals, hand-books issued by the Chamber of Commerce on local matters, small city street directories, and all such; they are paper-bound and they make no claim whatever to durability. They usually can't be bound, either, even if you felt like doing so, which you don't. Of its very nature this sort of thing is going to be quickly out-dated.

Yet it is manifestly silly to put such material through as is; you know that after two circulations they'll come back for repair, and that means a period during which they'll be unavailable to the public--which is a poor idea for books with such a short useful life.

You have two solutions.

One is to put such material into pamphlet-binders, using **LIGHT DILUTION** over the stickum provided on the hinges. This is recommended for the income-tax manuals, which will get a lot of hard wear; borrowers using them are apt to be in not the best of tempers. Of the civil-service study books, some are going to get more wear than others--the general tests, post-office clerk-carrier, fire and police, clerical and file clerk, janitor-custodian, and so on. These, too, should be protected at once by a pamphlet-binder.

In doing so, remove the paper casing altogether and give the backs-of-the-signatures a good coating of **HEAVY DILUTION**. You may then cut off the original front cover and attach it with **LIGHT DILUTION** to the outside of the front cover of the pamphlet-binder, pressing overnight. This extra touch, while not necessary, is pleasant.

As for the less-essential material, it can be prepared for limited circulation in a much simpler way. Cut a strip of book-cloth the exact length of the spine, and wide enough to lap over about a half inch onto each side-cover. Attach it firmly with **HEAVY DILUTION**. (An excellent idea is to, at the same time, remove the contents from the covers, coat the backs-of-the-signatures with **HEAVY DILUTION**, and replace the contents in the paper cover. This extra reinforcement will prove an admirable insurance policy.) Stickum-ed tape is very good for this purpose; indeed, it might well have been invented for the purpose--but put it on with **LIGHT DILUTION**. Naturally this should be done before the book is accessioned, so that one marking will serve. It's just extravagant to wait until the original spine is torn, since you know quite well that this is bound to happen.

If, by bad luck, the contents of such a book manages to get away from its casing

Anybody Can Do Anything

before you are ready to discard it, plain hinge tape front and back will probably hold it together for the necessary length of time.

MUSIC SCORES

Back in the brave old days, music scores--which are customarily cased in thin paper--were always bound immediately upon purchase. This certainly preserved them, but if any of you have ever tried to play a piece from such a bound score, you know the drawback. The foolish volume just won't stay open on the stand or rack, and you have to prop it with ash-trays, paper-weights, or maybe eyebrow tweezers or clothes-pins over the pages. The whole virtue of music is to stay open while you play or sing from it, and that is exactly what bound music will not do.

Add to that the gruesome price of music, plus the cost of binding, and it becomes obvious that it would be nice if we could think of a way to make music scores capable of circulating and easy to use, and still properly preserved against wear-and-tear.

It can be done--and without much trouble. Simply remove the contents from the paper covers--you can throw them away; they're rather dull usually--and insert the contents into a pamphlet-binder. But first, coat the backs-of-the-signatures thoroughly with **HEAVY DILUTION**, and reinforce with a strip of cheesecloth or other soft material lapped over a quarter-inch or so onto the first and last pages. When dry, wax and then put into the pamphlet-binder, using **LIGHT DILUTION** on the hinges. The result is a quite usable volume which will stay open on rack or stand, and also endure long years of use. One of the nice things about knowing this technique is that you can frequently pick up excellent bargains in slightly worn scores--those paper covers get shabby just hanging around a store--and fix them up as if they were brand new.

INSECTS

I have canvassed Southern libraries extensively in the hope of finding somebody who has any bright ideas for dealing with insects--the kind which eat books. Everyone I've been able to lure into correspondence agrees that fumigation is the only solution--fumigation and a nice, air-conditioned library specially designed to foil the little varmints. There is a general agreement that supplies and materials must be chosen with a careful eye on the dietary preferences of these undesired colleagues, and that while they love starch-based pastes and starch-filled book-cloth, they don't thrive so well on synthetics. But I don't need to tell a Southern librarian about this, and really I only mention it to show other librarians that they think <u>they</u>'ve got troubles!

But if anybody does have any suggestions......?

LEFT-OVER DILUTION

What, you inquire, about dilutions which are not all used up in one mending session?

Well, if you mean to work again within a day or two, simply lay a sheet of waxed paper (or, better, the clear plastic wrapping which I have previously mentioned, the stuff you use to wrap left-overs in your refrigerator) over the jar and clamp down the cover. Refrigerator-jars have well-fitting covers and the left-over dilution will remain usable for as much as a week. You can always add a little water, if necessary, when you start to work again.

But if you only mend at widely separated intervals, you may--if there is a lot left over--pour it back into the main supply bottle. (Only, of course, if it is neither discolored nor dirty.) The only time that I can think of when this would be necessary is when you have set yourself up to mend and are suddenly called away with no possibility of return. Usually, the small amount of dilution which is made up at a time gets itself used up and there's much

Anybody Can Do Anything

more likelihood of your having to make up two batches than of your having much left over. In the unlikely case that you positively have quite a portion, in pristine cleanliness, it can be poured back into the main supply jar and mixed in by shaking the bottle vigorously. It will simply add more water to the original viscosity, and your future dilutions will be regulated by your knowledge of this fact. If you use a large bottle for supply, it won't make a dickens of a lot of difference.

I've also been asked, on occasion, whether it is safe to pour the dregs of a dilution down the drain. So far as I know, it is; I haven't heard of anybody having trouble. But just on general principles, in case the plumbing is clogged or ancient, it's probably as well to use lots of water.

NOTE: Brushes which get coated with the plastic adhesive--the handles, that is--can be soaked until the coating turns white and then scrubbed clean with the wire suede brush, or scraped clean with a knife.

LIMP LEATHER

Limp-leather side-covers have a sorrowful way of cracking down the middle, although otherwise they wear quite well. There are two methods of dealing with this.

You can remove the limp-leather casing altogether, and substitute a new hard-cover casing, as directed in Chapters Nine and Ten. This is probably the best thing to do with minor classics, which don't get out of date.

For technical books, which do, and which often turn up in this guise, it will be sufficient to hold the side-covers together until the expected new edition comes out. For this, a strip of plain hinge attached with HEAVY DILUTION along the crack on the inside of the side-cover (and well waxed) will do. It won't look like much, but it will keep the book going for the necessary period.

GREASE SPOTS

Everybody thinks we're nuts, we poor librarians (they could, of course, be right, but not for this reason) when we mention the extraordinary things which people do to books. I've seen a book completely covered with fudge sauce; I have fished out bacon strips (medium crisp), lettuce leaves, bread crusts and old neckties used as bookmarks. The only thing nobody ever seems to use is a five-dollar bill, and this is very discouraging.

Admitting that it is a cardinal sin to dog-ear a book, some of these ways of avoiding that crime leave rather unlovely grease-marks. It is not very easy to remove them. In fact, it can't be done. But the stuff sold for getting rid of wax crayon is pretty good, and worth trying. A clean blotter under the page and a good soaking with the remover will take at least the worst of the grease out.

VARIOUS STAINS AND PROBLEMS

The black binding which holds together some of the transparent plastic protective covers for dust-jackets has one discouraging trait. If a borrower insists on storing his library books on a hot radiator, the goo in the black binding bleeds onto the book-cover underneath, and sometimes even onto the inner pages. When you finally discard the dust-jacket and cover, you have that black sticky rim around the book. It is not easy to remove. Alcohol is fairly effective--denatured, naturally--but better still is the solvent sold for removing wax crayon.

Many stains just don't explain themselves. Somebody may spill spaghetti on a book, or medicine, or French dressing. Or blood. A degree in chemical engineering would be handy for menders.

When confronted with a mysterious stain, try plain water first. Then denatured alcohol. Then any solvent you happen to have around. If that doesn't work, there won't, likely, be any paper left, either, and you can forget the whole project. There are times when the public has us licked.

FOXING

"Foxing" is the technical term for discoloration which happens to aging paper. It looks like the result of water-soaking, except that the edges of the stain are brownish. Not a thing can be done about it; it's the result of a chemical change in the paper itself, and in this case Time is not the Great Healer but the very disease. It doesn't look very pretty, but it will be quite some time before even a badly foxed page will disintegrate, so it's not necessary to discard a book which has begun to suffer from it. People who consult books old enough to be "foxed" usually know all about it; if they don't, they should.

SCIENCE MARCHES ON

You'll have observed, I think, that I'm not exactly a conservative type. I think Science is peachy, and I'm perfectly willing to try anything once. I'm the Salesman's Friend, I am.

Therefore, somebody is going to ask why I haven't mentioned some things which are currently on the market, and the answer is, usually, that I've tried 'em and didn't like them, for one reason or another. (There may be some I've missed, though, and if anyone cares to call them to my attention, I'll be delighted.)

The electric stylus, for instance. Some people can do satisfactory marking with it, quickly and easily. I am not one of them, which is probably my fault, and I prefer water-proof ink and fountain-pen instead. But I have no other objection to it than its requisite of absolute infallibility; me, I make mistakes and I like to be able to erase them quick-like before anybody notices.

Same way with the various holders for books during marking. No matter where I attach these to a desk, I manage to lose an inch of skin off my hip by walking into the gadget unwarily. And anyway, who needs a holder? Just open the front cover flat along the desk edge, or the edge of the pull-out shelf if your desk has one, so that the contents hangs down over your lap. The spine is flat and even with the desk-edge, just right for marking. What could be simpler? But I don't want to queer anybody's pitch, and if you like a holder, that's altogether up to you.

Again, book-lacquer or anything else put up in a pressurized can. Only here, my own distaste is reinforced by the voluble dislike of my colleagues. Pressurized squirt-cans were obviously devised by a masculine brain. The fine mist which shoots out of them does not confine itself to the target area. It spreads out all over, with a special affinity for hair and clothes. Not only do most such chemicals smell as if somebody were vulcanizing an old overshoe, they are definitely not good for the hair. So you can be as modern and efficient as you wish, but I'll stick to bottle-and-brush.

And so it goes. But the very next salesman who passes by may very well produce something stupendous and earth-shaking, and don't think I won't try it--if I can get the Front Office to buy me some to play with.

Chapter Sixteen
THE MYSTIQUE
or
Why Are Menders?

What makes a good teacher--of anything?

    a) knowledge of the subject

    b) enthusiasm

Training an assistant in book repair is no different from any other apprentice-teaching. You know how to mend; you know why it must be done. <u>And</u> you like doing it. Given these three essentials, you can readily train a staff--whether of one or twenty--who will rapidly become more mechanically skillful than you are, and thus leave you free for the enviable job of supervising, revising, and thinking up new ways and means of handling mending.

The first step is to convince the novice that mending books, far from being tedious and prosaic, is vital. This isn't hard, because it happens to be precisely true. A library which doesn't mend soon ceases to be more than unfair competition for the corner drug store rental collection; it is of no lasting value to the people who pay taxes to support it.

Our American people quite honestly expect that their library will be able to answer any question that pops into their heads--whether the question arises out of their work, or a bar-room argument, or a newspaper puzzle, or a TV quiz, or a philosophical doubt born in the course of insomnia. They have a perfect right to expect these answers, since they are our employers.

The maintenance of an adequate Reference Department won't altogether do it. People frequently want to take home a book and mull it over, or show it to a friend-- stabbing at the exact paragraph which proves their point. This, too, is a perfectly reasonable expectation.

You just never know what the next borrower will ask for. In the course of a single day you may be asked for the schematic of a spark-gap transmitter, the specifications of a 1945 Bugatti, a picture of the kepi of the French Foreign Legion in the Beau Geste period, the home-life of a vampire bat, how to make soap from left-over fat, a critique of Swedenborg, how to cook a sturgeon, the anatomy of a caterpillar, a picture of Chicago before the Great Fire, the construction of a strap-hung carriage with telegraph springs, and the lesser-known poems of Michael Drayton. All of these things, and millions more, have been in print at one time or another. Very few of them are available in books which can be purchased at this very moment in a book-store. They are out of print, and unless you have cherished and preserved the one book in which they appeared, you are a dead duck when the hopeful borrower turns to you with his touching--and tax-paid-- faith.

Why are Menders?

There's that, to argue for book-repair which never abandons a book if it's humanly possible to salvage it.

Then, there's this. Our public believes that we are a sort of community memory. The books they read in their childhood, the book they saw somewhere long ago and can just remember the title only they always meant to get around to reading it some day, the books they have heard recommended from the most unlikely sources-- these are the books they expect to find in their library, along with the current best-sellers. Every librarian who has been in the profession for any length of time has had at least one warming experience of having a borrower ask timidly for a book--quite likely one she never heard of--and when to her disguised surprise she finds it on the shelf and hands it over, having the borrower light up like a Christmas tree, exclaiming, "Say, I've been looking for this book in every library I've been in around the country, and none of them had it! This must be quite a library you've got here!"

Well, you don't get pleasant thrills like that unless your mending department is on the ball.

The first step in indoctrinating a prospective mender, then, is to impress upon her that a book--any book, every book--is a sometime thing. It doesn't reproduce itself every year like the birds. It comes once, and with a few exceptions, that's it. The easiest way to demonstrate this is to show her the serried volumes of the CBI--and then show her the current volume of Books in Print. Right then and there she loses her layman's notion that a worn-out book can easily be replaced, so why bother repairing, or even mourning over, a book chewed up by the family pup or left out on a deck-chair in the rain?

The next step is to show her your treasures--your most valuable books, beautifully and tenderly repaired-- and for such demonstration purposes, you might wisely keep one volume in its original state of disintegration, as a before-and-after object lesson. This won't impress her much at first, because she doesn't yet realize how much work and know-how have gone into the job, but it will show her what results are expected.

Then you start teaching, progressing from simple to difficult operations exactly as we have proceeded in this book.

And at a certain point she'll catch fire, if she's worth having around at all, and after that you just sit back and admire. There is only one rule, and that is never to be satisfied with less than perfection. Anyone who wants to can do first-class book repair these days. (But experiments, even when they don't wholly succeed, are to be encouraged. When a mender gets to experimenting, she's caught fire and you can congratulate yourself.)

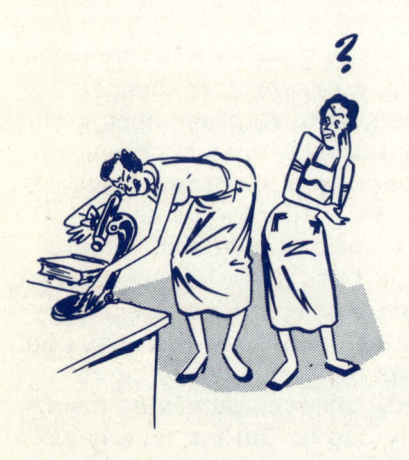

It takes about three months, on the average, to train a mender in all the techniques in this book, giving her sufficient practice on each to be letter-perfect and capable of improving on them as occasion offers. (This is considering that book-repair is rarely a full-time job.) For that training period, it will probably be wise to insist that these rules be followed precisely; after that, if your mender shows promise

Why are Menders?

and initiative, give her a free rein and let her improvise when she feels like it. Your job, then, is to think constructively about book-repair as it affects your particular collection, so that you'll have the answers when necessary. You'll do a great deal of experimenting yourself, naturally, and you'll read the trade papers, listen to salesmen, study advertising brochures, and try out everything you can persuade the Front Office to order for you. You'll cruise the stacks with a thoughtful eye, seeking those rarely-consulted o.p.'s which should be repaired before somebody takes them out and completes the ruin of time. No mended book goes back on the shelf until it has come under your personal scrutiny, and your standards shouldn't be just high, they should be absolute. (But don't raise Cain about an occasional sloppy job. Just hand it back to be done over. When you get more sloppy jobs than good ones, get rid of the mender; she's a menace to the collection, and the collection is your responsibility.) In short, you won't be unoccupied; one way or another, you'll find yourself as busy as a bird dog with two tails, and quite as happy.

That responsibility is, you see, no light one.

Take it seriously, and be willing to fight for it. Until a modern, enterprising, interested mender shows up in a library, book-repair tends to lie under the stigma of the dead years.

To begin with you'll have to fight for time, for budgets, for help, and most of all for recognition. But once you start producing--as you very easily can if you put your back into it--you become Cinderella in her transformed pumpkin. There isn't a Chief Librarian in the land who won't value and cherish an intelligent and enthusiastic mender above rubies. And rightly so. You'll be saving both money and books, and nobody else in the outfit is doing either, however valuable their work may be.

Yet that isn't the reason why book-repair today is a source of infinite satisfaction to those who practice it. The real reason is deeper and much more important.

You--your skill, your devotion, your ingenuity--are saving the collection for posterity. Your colleagues mostly serve today; you serve God knows how many unlikely tomorrows. You stand in a direct line with the monkish copyists who patiently preserved all that was left of the world's tradition of learning, and so brought Europe out of the Dark Ages. You, too, are preserving the Written Word against another and much darker age which can descend upon us this year, next year, some time. We pray that it won't happen, but we know all too well that it can. With the horrible mushroom of the bomb hanging over all our cities, who can dare to say that preserving even the smallest of collections in the most isolated of places isn't worth while?

One thing is sure. If the bomb ever gets loose from its tether, the great metropolitan collections are going to be one with the lost library at Alexandria. But somewhere, when the dust settles and what is left of us begins to

Why are Menders?

pick up the pieces of civilization, a small library whose mender has preserved every book she possibly could keep from dissolution may very well be the seed-bed of a new renaissance. Books are not expendable. Books must live--live physically, as their authors cannot--and <u>you</u> make it possible.

Be proud of your job, and enjoy it, and see beyond the clutter and dust and sticky brushes your reason for being. Few people in this modern world have a better one.

Chapter Seventeen
DO-IT-YOURSELF
or
Why EVERYBODY Needs This Book

Lots of people own books.

They inherit them, or acquire them by gift at Christmas, or in extreme cases even buy them for real money.

If you are thus the possessor of a private library, you may be interested to know that you can keep it in admirable shape your own self.

Your only problem will be to get hold of the plastic adhesive. Some book stores carry it, in a reluctant and surprised way, and if you look long enough and with sufficient insistence, you can likely get hold of a bottle. (One of these days a manufacturer will, I hope, put out a good kit for the mending of books at home; it appears, from the number of people who come into libraries seeking advice on how to fix the family Bible or a volume of an encyclopedia which has fallen on evil days, that there might be a small but genuine market for such a thing. Book-repair at home is at least as much fun as ceramics, and a lot less dangerous than a power-saw.)

But don't confuse the polyvinyl acetate emulsion which, for lack of a better generic term, we have called "plastic adhesive" with the various types of resin-base or casein-base glues on the market. These new glues are also white and viscous, and they are very good glues, but they are not nearly the miracle-workers that the plastic adhesive is, and moreover they haven't been specially developed for book repair. Your own library might be persuaded to give you a list of brand names and suppliers, through which your book store could track the stuff down for you.

Everything else you need you can easily provide for yourself. In Chapter Three you'll find directions for making your own hinge-tape (and I suggest surgical gauze bandage as the easiest to use; you won't after all be needing a great deal of it, so economy is not the factor that it is for a library.) Brushes abound in artists'-supply stores. Everything else you probably have around the house anyway.

(Except, perhaps, a bone. Bones are used in offices which go in for form letters and direct-mail advertising, so presumably they can be found in stationery stores. Or ask your library to show you a bone; once you've seen one, you may be able to think of an adequate substitute. The spine of a plastic pocket comb, for instance, or a heavy, smooth letter-opener.)

Now as to backing material. Any fairly heavy fabric will do; books for private libraries have often been backed, or even cased, in brocade, linen, light tapestry, sail-cloth, and even burlap. A remnant shop ought to provide an ample supply of decorative and attractive materials. Or you can try an upholsterer's shop for the lightest-weight imitation leather--this makes a

Why EVERYBODY Needs This Book 131

spectacularly handsome job.

As for treating those leather-bound sets which Aunt Mimosa left you in her will instead of the real estate which you hoped for, Chapter Fourteen lists the necessary materials as well as the method of using them, and you can buy enough to do fifty volumes for considerably less than a dollar. If you're going to keep the things around, they might as well look good--and indeed, few decorations for a living room are as handsome and, these days, unusual as a serried row of classics which smell delightful and have the soft, authentic gleam of polished leather.

Just to demonstrate some of the possibilities of book-repair as a home craft, we'll go into specific examples:

TEXT BOOKS

Students, if they have any sense, buy their texts second-hand--which frequently means fifth-hand at least. If they are to be turned in for cash or credit at the end of the year, it will pay dividends to reinforce them. A very small investment in time and materials will easily repair a pile of texts so securely that they'll last the year without appreciable damage and be perfectly saleable in June.

CHILDREN'S BOOKS

Considering the price of books for youngsters these days, any parent ought to be willing to put in a little time repairing the inevitable damage. (PLEASE, don't practice on library or school books! You can have ample fun with the books which your child actually owns.) For instance, those lovely illustrated volumes which fond relatives come through with at Christmas and birthdays. It's a shuddersome spectacle to watch such expensive beauties being read by a child hung upside down over the back of a sofa or sprawled happily among the petunias. But nothing is more daunting to a potential bookworm than to be "allowed" to read only with washed hands and in a solemn spirit. He'll be back to the comics in no time.

Consequently, the instructions in Chapters Eleven and Twelve ought to come in handy. There's nothing in the least complicated there, and indeed any child of twelve ought to be able to follow them and probably enjoy it. You yourself can easily repair any broken-down book for the toddlers. Knowing this, you can let the sprouts read as and how they please--and such a free-and-easy attitude may possibly have a good effect on little Johnnies who are not taking to books with any enthusiasm. I know I practically ruined every book in my father's library because I preferred to read them up in a pear tree, and they inevitably fell down even before I did. My father endured this with what I now recognize as amazing stoicism, sensibly preferring a battered library to an illiterate child, but if he'd known how to fix the poor victims we could both have been happy.

LEGAL AND MEDICAL PRIVATE COLLECTIONS

Lawyers and doctors customarily have valuable libraries, often bound in solid leather, which cost the devil and all. To allow them to deteriorate on the shelves is a great waste. Chapter Fourteen indicates how such handsome volumes can be preserved in excellent condition, so that they can be handed down or sold in due time, or even become a desirable bequest to the local library,

Why EVERYBODY Needs This Book   133

complete with commemorative bookplates. (A doctor or lawyer who thinks well of this notion might inquire of a neighboring library; a mender there might agree to handle the job on her vacation or in her spare time.)

OTHER PROFESSIONAL LIBRARIES

Lots of men these days--architects, engineers, technicians, and so on--find themselves necessarily acquiring a small but expensive library just to keep up with their work. These volumes range from technical works required by engineers in all the various fields to the manuals used by repair technicians for TV and other intricate electrical apparatus. They represent an investment, and in many cases get a deuce of a lot of hard wear as well. No matter what the format of such books, they can be repaired by one or other of the techniques herein described. If you have anyone in this category in the family, it might be a kindly thought to draw attention to this possibility.

CITY AND TOWN HALLS

Records preserved in ledgers or looseleaf folders can easily be made into permanent volumes, following the directions in Chapter Fifteen.

MUSICIANS

Music scores are hideously expensive. And not only do they cost like sixty, they come in paper casings which do not last very well. (And that's an understatement!).

But it's really quite easy to reinforce any type of score so that it will last, and at the same time preserve its great virtue of staying open on the rack or stand.

Simply remove the paper casing entirely. Coat the backs-of-the-signatures with plastic adhesive, and then cover the backs-of-the-signatures with a strip of cheesecloth sufficiently wide to lap over perhaps a quarter of an inch on either side. (Bandage will do nicely, but if you are a professional musician and have a sizable library, get several yards of cheesecloth and cut it into suitable strips; it'll be much cheaper.) Thereafter, you can attach the paper casing again just by coating the inside of the cover-spine with plastic adhesive and fitting cover and contents together.

If you want a job which will last a lifetime, though, consult Chapters Eight and Nine. Chapter Eight will tell you how to attach paper side-covers permanently, and in Chapter Nine are instructions for putting on a durable fabric back. If you wish, you can make the fabric extend right to the edges of the side covers, trimming it even and not endeavoring to fold it over as you would do when re-casing hard-covers. Attach the fabric to the covers with plastic adhesive and press under ample weight for a day or two. (Reinforcing the side-covers with cardboard is not recommended, since music is rarely put together with the essential "ledge".)

Sheet music will profit by immediate reinforcement along the fold. The permanent mending tape is good for this, or a narrow strip of cheesecloth attached with plastic adhesive. The permanent mending tape can also be used effectively to keep the pages of a selection on which you are going to be working for a long period from growing thin and tearing. Just run a strip down the inside of the page-edge so that constant turning won't hurt it. (This treatment should not be extended to all the pages, though; it will create too much bulk.)

Orchestra-librarians may like the idea of making "the book" into a genuine volume, after the directions in Chapter Thirteen, since the method is precisely the same as that used to make periodicals into usable books. This will

Why EVERYBODY Needs This Book   135

insure that the first trumpet won't be forever losing the lead-sheet on "Take the A-Train" and when the alto sax feels like pitching the book at the leader, he'll have something substantial to throw--which you won't have to pick up and reassemble afterwards. (I've been there; I know.)

SECOND-HAND BOOKS

About the selling of second-hand books I know as little as is humanly possible. I do know a bit about the buying end, since the sight of a table marked "Any book here, 25¢" affects me like a neon saloon sign a fugitive from AA. But the inwardness of the trade is--so to speak-- a closed book. All I know is that first editions mustn't be tampered with, or if possible even read; otherwise they lose value.

But it occurs to me that I have in my time acquired some bargains because the book in question lacked a spine or was otherwise in need of repair. True, even so I bought the book, but being New England born I chaffered the price down first. Had it been in good repair I'd likely have had to spring for an extra fifty cents to get it.

So I wonder, mildly, if book-sellers might not find the techniques herein suggested useful? Chapter Fourteen on the treatment of leather naturally leaps to the mind, but even more hopeful, I should think, might be the quick and simple procedures recommended in Chapter Five. These two techniques will put a not-too-badly battered book into practically mint condition in a couple of minutes--and they don't show.

Moreover, it might well pay second-hand booksellers to secure and place on sale some of the plastic adhesive--both the kind made specially for treating leather and the kind developed especially for mending books. Together, of course, with copies of this book (Advertisement) so that customers who wish to restore a set of the eleventh edition of the Britannica or a badly-dried-out full-calf edition of Croker's Boswell may be encouraged to go home and do so. Most people who frequent second-hand bookstalls like to fool around with books, and they could very likely be induced to buy some thoroughly beat-up specimens if they could be assured that a little pleasant work would put their purchases into readable and good-looking shape. The beauty of this sales-talk is that it is quite true.

HOUSEHOLD FILES

The keeping of scrap-books by housewives is universal. Usually their clippings from newspapers and magazines are mounted in ten-cent-store scrapbooks which are not specially durable. When, after a few years, these precious collections begin to tear loose, any housewife can easily make the pages into a fairly durable volume by following the instructions in Chapter Fifteen for the reconstructing of looseleaf folders and albums. Any attractive fabric of reasonable weight can be used to make backs for the new "books" and it can be matched to the kitchen color-scheme. Similarly, that treasured cookbook which "his" mother learned to cook from can be salvaged and kept as a family heirloom, and your own well-worn, cherished cookery bible can just as

Why EVERYBODY Needs This Book 137

well have a nice new cover--light-weight oil-cloth is sensible and pretty--whenever it needs it.

POCKET-SIZE PAPER-BACKS

These days, for everybody who buys a hard-cover book, there are fifty who invest in one of the small paper-covered volumes in which so much admirable material is re-printed (and even issued originally.) For one thing, these paper-backs are inexpensive, and for another--just as important in these days of restricted living space--you can assemble quite a respectable library of such books in a couple of bookcases. Trouble is, the backs come off very easily.

Given some plastic adhesive, this is easily cured. Simply detach the cover completely, and coat the backs-of-the-signatures with plastic adhesive. When it is dry, paint the inside of the cover-spine with plastic adhesive and fit the contents back in. Put the book under a pile of real books, or a brick, and allow to dry overnight. You'll be astonished how much hard wear your paper-backs will take after this simple treatment.

If you have neglected to do this until the spine has become torn, a coat of plastic adhesive on the <u>outside</u> of the spine will hold the torn sections together almost invisibly. But in this case, it will be wise to apply a light coat of colorless shoe polish or leather cream after the plastic has dried transparent--or you can rub the spine vigorously with household wax (paraffin) or a white candle. Otherwise there is some danger that the book may stick to its neighbors on the shelf.

When the spine has vanished entirely, you can easily improvise a new back. Simply cover with a strip of some fairly heavy material--moire´ or taffeta ribbon, linen, even chintz--attached to about half an inch of the adjoining side-covers with plastic adhesive. You can then type or letter a strip of paper with the author and title and attach it to the new spine. To prevent this paper label from discoloring or getting blurred, run a light coat of plastic adhesive <u>over</u> it and when the plastic has dried, wax it.

I have heard of some industrious bibliophiles who have used very light-weight imitation leather, such as upholsterers sell, to make not just new spines but complete new covers for the most valuable of their paper-backs. (It is not advisable to try to reinforce the side-covers with cardboard. Paper-backs are not made with the vital "ledge" and so a heavier cover will inevitably tear the signatures loose.) But simply covering the whole book with a neat new cover-cloth of light-weight imitation leather, trimmed even with the edges of the side cover and not attached to the actual spine, creates something quite like a "limp-leather" volume (and has the additional virtue of obliterating the often-regrettable front cover, which is often right out of Krafft-Ebbing even when the contents are pure Santayana or Croce.) I'd recommend, if this scheme appeals to you, reinforcing the junction of contents and side-covers, inside the book, with hinges of cheesecloth or surgical gauze bandage. These are put in according to the instructions for putting in plain hinge in Chapter Eight.

Paper labels can then be affixed, as mentioned in the previous paragraph. But if you can print legibly, and intend to do a number of books, you may be interested to ask your local library for the address of a firm making waterproof marking ink and a suitable pen--ordinary white ink, unless protected by lacquer or shellac, tends to blur in handling.

As you can readily see, a project like this could easily entertain a bibliomaniac for many a long winter evening, at the most minor expense. I commend it to wives whose husbands are restlessly beginning to eye the power-tool ads. Hardly anyone has ever

Why EVERYBODY Needs This Book   139

landed in the hospital from repairing a book.

FINALE

    I haven't been able to think of any reason why a steeple-jack, a lobsterman, or a pearl-diver should need this book.

    Otherwise.....

    So go and beseige your bookstores. Eventually a manufacturer will supply you with the necessary materials. Free Enterprise responds to a "felt want" and even if you haven't felt it up to now, I trust that by this time you are practically frothing.

    Have fun. I have; I know *you* will.

GLOSSARY

BACK--another term for "spine", which see

BACK SIDE COVER--the side-cover which protects the last page of the contents

BACKING--technical term for replacing a spine

BASIC COLLECTION--the books which a library must keep on hand to satisfy public demand, including classics, texts and definitive works in all fields

BINDER--1) a man who binds books; 2) a card-board-and-fabric casing into which unbound or paper-covered material may be fitted by means of inner hinges, known as a pamphlet-binder; 3) a larger version of (2) designed to hold a year's issues of a magazine, known as a magazine binder; 4) double-stitched binder, a combination of hinges-and-spine-liner designed for the re-casing of books.

BINDING--1) the protective covering of a book, to be distinguished from "casing", which is the modern machine-method of achieving the same end; 2) the process of putting the "contents" of a book into a binding or casing; 3) in general speech, the process of removing the original binding or casing of a book and replacing it with a new one--this should properly be termed re-binding or re-casing; also the process of placing unbound material into a binding or casing, as pamphlets or periodicals

BLEEDING--1) loss of color from dyed cloth when wet;

2) oozing or melting of adhesive from under treated tape or fabric
BONE--a flat piece of ivory, bone or plastic with blunted edges and curved ends, designed to smooth paper or cloth without tearing (also known as a BONE FOLDER, FOLDING BONE)
BOOK-BINDER'S SAW--special saw with very fine teeth
BOOK CLOTH--buckram or some similar fabric, designed for the binding or casing of books
BOOK REPAIR--mending a book
BROWN PAPER--heavy-weight brown wrapping paper

CASING--machine-method of placing the contents of a book into a protective covering (see BINDING)
CHEESECLOTH--coarsely woven cloth (see SUPER and SURGICAL GAUZE BANDAGE)
CONCENTRATION--a term for the ratio of solids to liquid in a dilution or emulsion (see VISCOSITY)
CONTENTS--the whole of the signatures of a book; the printed text, title page, etc.
COVER-CLOTH--a term for the original covering of a book (it can be paper) which conceals the side-covers and forms the spine. Nowadays it is usually a light fabric; it was originally leather, and has in history been almost everything from canvas to vellum and cloth-of-gold
CPS--one one-hundredth of a poise, the unit of viscosity. See POISE, VISCOSITY
CREASE--the indented grooves on either side of the spine, at the point where the spine meets the side-covers; designed to provide a little "play" for the covers so that they can open and close without straining the signatures; the outward indication of the "ledge", which see

GLOSSARY

CROPPING--cutting off a small portion of a page or pages along the outer edge

DENSITY--term for the ratio between solids and liquid in a dilution or emulsion (see CONCENTRATION, VISCOSITY)

DILUTION--solid material mixed with liquid, or a heavy concentration thinned with liquid

DUST JACKET--the decorative illustrated paper cover provided by the publisher to protect a book from handling, and also to make it more attractive

END-PAPERS--heavy stock, sometimes beautifully mapped or decorated, used as lining for the inside of side-covers and extending to form front and back fly-leaves. Practically, they serve as reinforcements for the "super" which makes the hinge connecting contents and casing

FALSE TITLE PAGE--an extra page sometimes attached to the inside of the front end paper, upon which may appear simply the title of the book, or which may be left blank

FEATHERED--term for a tear in paper which has soft, irregular edges, as distinguished from a clean cut or slash

FOLDER, BONE--see BONE

FOLDING BONE--see BONE

FOXING--technical term for discoloration which occurs in aging paper; it resembles water-staining but is usually brownish, and results from a chemical change in the paper itself

FRONT SIDE COVER--the side-cover which protects the first page of the contents

FUMIGATION--process adopted in libraries to get rid of insects injurious to books; in some cases a special room is set aside for the purpose, in other cases whole departments are fumigated by professional experts

GLUE--the traditional end of Dobbin, or anyway his bones and hooves. Modern glues are apt to be based on various types of plastic, resin, casein, etc.

HARD-COVER--term designating a book cased in stiff covers, as distinguished from books whose covers are paper, thin card-board or limp-leather
HINGE--1) the juncture between side-covers and contents; 2) cloth or paper employed to reinforce the hinge-juncture
HINGE-TAPE--cloth designed to reinforce hinge-junctures

INDUSTRIAL WASTE CLOTH--remnants of soft cloth sold in bulk to factories, garages, filling stations and other places where cheap and disposable cloth is required in quantity
INSECTS--book-worms, cigarette beetles, silver-fish, and various other forms of insect life which feed on leather, paper, paste and glue and thus deface or destroy books

JUVENILE--technical term in library work for a book written for children

LACQUER--transparent liquid designed to waterproof and protect the covers of books (see SHELLAC)
LEDGE--the lip formed along each edge of the backs of the signatures of a book, by heavy pressure during the original binding or casing process; it permits the side-covers to open and close easily without putting a strain on the signatures
LEGAL TAPE--soft, narrow tape, usually red, designed for tying documents into bundles without damage; the origin of the phrase "red tape"
LIMP LEATHER--very light-weight leather, usually simulated, used as a casing for small books or books printed on very thin paper; in place of side-covers, the leather itself is reinforced by layers of heavy paper

GLOSSARY 145

MAGAZINE BINDER--see BINDER

MENDING--book repair in general

MENDING TAPE--a transparent pressure tape developed by the makers of the more familiar Scotch tape, intended for the permanent repair of documents, book pages and all types of paper

MILDEW--a greenish mould propagated by dampness, similar to yeast, penicillin and the mycins but of no known use to science and particularly apt to form on paper, cloth and leather when wet

MITRE--a way of folding fabric or paper neatly over a corner; the fold is triangular, roughly like a bishop's mitre. Also spelled "miter"

ONION SKIN--a thin, tough, semi-transparent paper, often used for tracing and for fourth and fifth carbons

PAMPHLET BINDER--see BINDER

PAPER-BACKS--somewhat inaccurate trade term for pocket-sized editions which are actually cased in thin card-board side-covers, with very light-weight slick paper acting as "cover-cloth." Fifty years ago in this country, and even now on the Continent, many regular editions were actually cased in thin paper, it being expected that the purchaser would have the contents bound to match his personal collection. The present pocket-edition paper-back is quite a different matter, but the term remains a convenient way of distinguishing such books from "hard cover" editions

PLAIN HINGE TAPE--a strip of fabric designed to reinforce the hinge-juncture of a book

PLASTIC ADHESIVE--an arbitrary general term to designate emulsions of polyvinyl acetate, which see

PLASTIC WRAPPING--clear plastic sold in rolls or sheets for wrapping left-overs in a refrigerator

POISE--the unit of viscosity, expressed as one dyne per second per square centimeter, and aren't you sorry you asked? Viscosity, which see, is usually expressed in hundredths of a poise, mercifully abbreviated to cps

POLYETHELENE--a plastic used to make flexible, unbreakable bottles and containers

POLYVINYL ACETATE--a plastic polymer of vinyl acetate, a chemical formed from acetylene and acetic acid. It has an infinity of uses in industry, and among these is the production of a versatile, tough, quick-drying adhesive when mixed with water and various additives. Each manufacturer has his own formula, and because the product is comparatively new, it is still in the process of adaptation and improvement for the especial requirements of book repair. It is sold as an emulsion, white, viscous and water-soluble. It dries almost transparent, but retains its ability to absorb water. The amount of water used in making any given brand regulates the viscosity of the product. (See VISCOSITY)

PRE-BOUND BOOKS--regular editions of juveniles re-cased in more durable coverings for the use of libraries

PRESS, BOOK--a vise, provided with heavy press-board leaves, in which books may be dried under pressure

RE-CASING--replacing the original casing of a book

REFRIGERATOR-JARS--plastic jars intended for the storing of left-overs in the domestic refrigerator, or the similar jars provided for freezers

RONDURE--the curve produced in a group of signatures (which see) by shaping them under pressure to produce the "ledge" (which see) so that the backs of the signatures have a concave curve, while the fore-edge--the edge of the pages--has a concave shape. Only signatures so shaped can be successfully bound or cased in hard-covers.

SETS--groups of volumes in matched bindings, or casings. Often the "collected works" of a single author. The spine is ordinarily covered in leather--or something that looks like it--and the rest of the side-covers in marbled or decorative paper.

GLOSSARY

SHELLAC--a colorless preparation for the protection of book-covers from water and handling. See LACQUER

SIDE-BOARDS--another term for side-covers

SIDE-COVERS--stiff protective covers placed at the front and back of the book, held together by the spine and attached to the contents by the super and endpapers. Nowadays side-covers are usually made of cardboard of varying weight; originally they were flat pieces of wood or even metal (as ship's code-books in war-time are still sheathed in lead so that in case of imminent capture they can be tossed overside and be sure to sink.)

SIGNATURE--a group of folded pages, one inside the other, stitched together. All the signatures together make up the "contents" of a book. The number of pages so folded together may vary; usually there are eight, twelve, or sixteen. The most plausible explanation of the term dates back to the days of hand-copied books. Monks in Scriptoria, the monastery copy-rooms, received a group of folded pages of vellum or parchment, upon which to copy a similar amount of text. When this was done, they handed back the finished work and received another group of blank pages. Since it would be necessary for the Master of the Scriptorium to collate the work with the original book and, when necessary, raise holy cain about mistakes, it was customary for the copyist to affix his signature or a symbol at the end of each block of finished pages. It's easy to imagine that when the monks filed out of the silent Scriptorium at the end of the day for a few minutes relaxation in the cloister, one of them might well say to another, "Well, how many signatures did you get through today?" In any case, the term has come down through all the changes in book-making, even though now a "signature" is actually one large sheet upon which many pages of print are run off through the presses, thereafter being folded, cut and stitched so that the pages follow each other in proper order. Signatures are held together by glue under a strip of coarse cheesecloth known as "super", which see

SPINE--the strip of "cover-cloth" separating the two side-covers, designed to fit exactly over the rondure of the backs-of-the-signatures, and upon which appear the title, author, publisher's imprint, etc.

STITCHED HINGE TAPE--two strips of plain hinge tape, sewn together down the center

STITCHING--1) the thread with which the separate pages of a signature are sewn together; 2) the line of stitching down the center of stitched hinge tape

STOCK--the paper upon which the contents of a book is printed. Nowadays it is made, usually, of pulped wood, which is why the Androscoggin River smells the way it does. Stock varies in weight, surface and color; the smoother, whiter and heavier it is, the more expensive and the longer it is apt to last. Rag-paper stock, which is astronomically expensive these days, was formerly common and accounts for the long life of books printed several centuries ago. But all paper stock, no matter what, will eventually become discolored and brittle just by the action of time

SUEDE BRUSH--a small hand-brush with wire bristles, designed to raise the nap on suede but useful for cleaning paste brushes upon which plastic adhesive has been allowed to harden. A wire kitchen brush or even a sturdy fine-toothed comb will often serve as well

SUPER--technical term in book-making for coarse cheese-cloth glued across the backs-of-the-signatures and extended about an inch onto each side-cover to form hinges

TITLE PAGE--introductory page of the contents, carrying the book title, author's name, publisher's imprint, etc.

VISCOSITY--the internal friction or resistance to change of form of a liquid. The thickness of a liquid or emulsion with respect to flow, the opposite of fluidity. It is expressed as a certain number of hundredths of

GLOSSARY

of poise, the unit of viscosity, abbreviated to cps.

WAX--ordinary household wax (paraffin) or white candle wax, used to waterproof any surface which has been treated with plastic adhesive so that in the event of high humidity, wet weather or an inadvertent dunking the plastic adhesive will not stick to a neighboring surface

WATER PROOFING--1) treating cloth which has a tendency to bleed with lacquer or shellac; 2) waxing any plastic-adhesive-treated surface; 3) coating leather with colorless polish

INDEX

Acetic acid--110
Albums
   phonograph--105ff
   looseleaf--105, 136
    reference clippings--105
Alcohol, denatured--108ff (for water damage), 116
Applicator jar--16
Architects--133
Art Books--106
Art gum--12, 43
Assembly line technique--31, 55, 64, 98
Atmospherics (see also weather)
   effect on plastic adhesive--6, 34, 41, 51, 56, 79
   effect on bookmobile collection--87

Back--2, 60, 61, 62, 65, 83, 105, 134, 137, 141
Back cover--1, 50
Backing
   colors, selection of--66
   how to--**30**, 31, 59ff, 137
   materials, selection of--17ff
   substitute materials--130
Backing material
   commercial--17ff, 66
   improvised--130, 136-7
Backing tape--84, 86, 87, 112
Backs-of-signatures--3, 7, 21, 22, 37, 38, 39, 50, 53, 54, 55, 57, 62, 63, 64, 71, 82, 83, 112, 113, 134, 137
Ball point ink--43
Bandage, surgical gauze--21, 130, 134, 138
Basic collection--9
Batiste--21
Best-sellers--9
Bibliophiles--138
Bind--see Re-casing
Binder, magazine--91, 93, 141
Binder, pamphlet--91, 105, 111, 112, 113
Binder, ring--103ff

INDEX

Bindery--9, 89, 103, 113
Binding--1, 10, 59, 60
Bleach--43
Bleeding
   of cover cloth--1, 47, 68 (onto page edges)
   of mending tape--17
   of plastic protective covers--116
Bond, typewriter--47, 71 (end-paper substitute), 84
Bone--15, 17, 33, 39, 41, 51, 55, 65, 71, 72, 130
Bone folder--see Bone
Book-binder's cord--92
Book-binder's saw--92
Book cloth
   colors, selection of--66
   storage--27
   types--17ff
   use--27, 60, 62, 63, 64, 65, 66, 69, 70, 71, 83, 112
Book-ends--91
Book lacquer--18, 47, 79, 110, 118, 138
Bookmobile--75, 87ff
Books in Print--123
Borrowers
   active--52
   art-loving--103
   butter-fingered--4
   gossipy--36
   hopeful--122
   larcenous--103
   timid--123
   virtuous--85
Bound books--1, 95
Bound magazines--89
Bound music--113
Branch libraries--75
Book-press--12, 53, 68, 90ff, 104, 108, 109
Brittle paper--10
Brown paper--12, 14, 27, 33, 62-64, 69, 70, 71, 106
Brush, suede--12, 14, 115
Bubbles--65, 108
Buckling--65
Buckram--59

INDEX

Calf--see Leather
Candle, white--14, 137
Case One--50ff
Case Two--50, 52ff
Cased books--1, 95, 96, 113
Casein base glue--130
Casing--1, 2, 3, 4, 37, 47, 52, 53, 67ff, 82, 83, 84, 86, 92 (magazines), 108, 109, 115 (limp leather)
CBI (Cumulative Book Index)--123
Cheesecloth
 plain--13, 76, 104, 113, 134, 138
 super--3, 4, 21, 37, 40, 50, 52, 53, 63
Children's books (see also Juveniles)--19, 75, 77, 81ff (repair of), 131 (home repair)
City Hall records--133
Civil service handbooks--111ff
Clippings--107
Cloth, book--see Book Cloth
Cloth, industrial waste--12, 13, 33, 104
Colorless shoe polish--97, 100, 137
Colors, book cloth--66
Contents--1, 2, 3, 4, 29, 37, 39, 40, 41, 45, 50-56, 63, 65, 67, 68, 69, 71, 78, 82, 83, 85, 95, 108, 109, 112, 113, 137, 138
Cook books--136-7
Coping saw--92
Cover cloth--4, 13, 61, 62, 63, 65, 66, 95, 108, 109, 138
Covers
 original--29, 108, 109, 138
 plastic protective--31, 47, 60, 116
Crayon--43, 78, 116
Crayon remover--see Crayon
Crease--38, 39, 41, 59, 63, 65, 69, 71
Cropping--83
Custodians--13, 92, 103

Denatured alcohol--108ff, 116
Diagrams--45
Dilutions (see also Heavy dilution and Light dilution)

INDEX

   how to make
      heavy--34-5, 76
      light--34
   leftover--114
   why make--35, 77
Discarded covers--68, 105
Discards--5, 9
Discoloration
   of plastic adhesive--35, 77, 114
   of paper (foxing)--117
Discount--27ff
Do-it-yourself--60, 67, 129ff
Do-it-yourself manuals--60
Dogs--37, 67, 123
Double-flap--56-7
Double-stitched binder--21
Drawing paper--71
Dressmaker tape--21
Drying time (see also Weather)--41, 51, 53, 56
Duplicate copies--66

End-papers--3, 4, 20, 30, 40ff, 43, 50, 51, 52, 53, 71ff,
  79, 82
Engineers--133
Eraser--12
Erasing--31
Evaporation--36, 77
Exacto-knife--15, 61, 109

False title page--4
Feathered tears--44
First editions--135
Flap
  hinge--55ff, 83, 85ff
  double--56-7
  wedge-shaped--64, 70
Floods--37, 107ff
Folder, bone--see Bone
Folding bone--see Bone
Foxing--117
Freezing--16, 27

Front cover--1, 50, 138
Fumigation--114

Gauze--see Bandage, surgical gauze
Gilt pressure tape--19
Glue
   casein-base--130
   ordinary--5, 6, 7, 37, 38, 40, 49, 50, 52, 61, 62, 82, 88
   resin-base--130
Grease marks--116
Groove--see Crease
Gummed paper tape--15, 63

Hard-cover books--111, 137
Heavy dilution--34, 36, 38, 40, 44, 50, 53, 62, 64, 65, 82
   85, 104, 106, 109, 111, 115
Hinge--6, 7, 14, 21, 22, 30, 33, 35, 52, 54, 55, 56, 62, 72,
   78, 82, 83, 85, 113, 115, 138
Hinge tape
   double-stitched--21ff
   existing--19ff
   ideal--20
   how to make--21ff, 130
   how to use
       plain--21, 50ff, 113, 115, 138
       stitched--21, 54ff, 82, 83, 85, 105
   paper--22ff, 40
Holders, marking--118
Home book repair--129ff
Household wax--see Waterproofing wax
Housewives--136
Humidity (see also Weather)--34, 41, 87-8

Illustrations
   art plates--106
   tipping in--45
Imitation leather--131, 138
Income-tax manuals--111ff
Industrial waste cloth--12, 13 (description), 33, 36, 104
Ink eradicator--43
Ink, marking--see Marking

INDEX

Ink, removal--43
Ink, waterproof marking--18, 118, 138
Insects--114

Janitor--13, 92, 103
Jars
   applicator--16
   refrigerator--13, 34, 114
   use--12, 13, 34, 36, 76, 90, 98
Jj's--82
Juveniles (see also Children's books)--19, 75, 77, 79, 81ff,
   131 (home repair)

Knife-sharpener--12
Knives
   paring--12, 13, 53, 62, 115
   Exacto--15, 61, 109

Labels, paper--91, 93, 99, 137, 138
Lacquer, book--see Book Lacquer
Lead sheets--135
Leaks--107ff
Leather
   genuine--59, 89, 95ff, 108, 110, 132, 135
   imitation--131ff, 138
   sets--100, 131
Leather, limp--115, 138
Leather cream, neutral--97, 100, 137
Ledge--4, 20, 37, 40, 41, 51, 53, 55, 57, 63, 71, 72, 79,
   104, 134, 138
Ledgers--105
Left-over dilution--114
Legal libraries, private--132
Legal tape--92
Light dilution--34, 35, 36, 54, 55, 56, 63, 70, 72, 83, 84,
   86, 87, 91, 104, 106, 111
Light love stories--9
Limp leather--115, 138
Looseleaf binders--105, 136

INDEX

Mazaine binder--91
Magazines--89ff, 134
Magazines, bound--89ff
Manuals, repair--133
Maps--45
Marbled paper--96
Marked-up pages--43
Marking--18, 60, 112, 138
Marking-holders--118
Marking-ink, waterproof--18, 118, 138
Medical libraries, private--132
Menders--25ff, 121ff (training of)
Mending departments--11, 25ff, 122ff
Mending tape--see Permanent mending tape
Microfilming--107
Mildew--107ff
Minor repairs--43ff
Mitre--71
Music--111, 113ff, 133ff
Mysteries--9

Neat's foot oil--97ff, 108
Neutral leather cream--97, 100, 137
Newspapers
   discarded, use as working surface--12, 33, 76, 98
   repair of--106
Newsprint--106

Onion skin--see Paper
Opera scores--see Music
Orchestra librarians--133-4
Ordering supplies--27-8
Organ scores--see Music
Out-of-print--72, 111, 122
Over-sized juveniles--19, 82
Overlapping--57

Page edges, stained--68
Pages
   defaced--47, 85
   detachable--106

INDEX

    human--25ff, 121ff
    loose--14, 45
    lost--47, 85
    torn--15, 31, 44ff, 78, 84-5
Pamphlet binder--91, 105, 111-2, 113
Paper
    bond--47, 71, 84
    drawing paper--10
    foxing--117
    life expectancy--95
    pulp--95
    rag--95
Paper-bound books (see also Paper-covered books)--111ff, 137ff
Paper, brittle--10, 95
Paper-covered books--62, 66, 84
Paper cutter--12, 14, 19, 68, 83, 104
Paper hinge--7, 22, 40
Paper, waxed--see Waxed paper
Paper, wrapping--see Brown paper
Paraffin--see Wax, Waterproofing
Paring knife--12, 13, 53, 62, 115
Paste--5, 6, 7, 40, 61, 88, 106
Pen, marking--18, 60, 112, 138
Pencil marks--43
Pencil, red--12, 19, 63
Percale--21, 28
Periodicals--89ff, 134
Permanent mending tape--15, 17, 44, 76, 84, 106, 107, 134
Pets--67, 68
Phonograph albums--106ff
Picture books--57, 82-3
Pipes, leaking--107ff
Plain hinge tape--21, 50ff, 113, 115, 138
Plastic adhesive (see also Heavy dilution, Light dilution)--6, 7, 15, 27, 33, 34, 35, 36, 38, 39, 40, 41, 44, 45, 47, 51, 52, 54, 55, 61, 76, 78, 79, 88, 89, 90, 91, 92, 93, 97, 98, 99, 100, 101 (for leather), 106, 115, 129, 134, 136, 137
Plastic covers, protective--31, 47, 60, 116
Plastic wrapping--36, 114

Plates--45, 106, 108
Pocket-sized paper-backs--137ff
Polish, colorless shoe--97, 100, 137
Polyethylene containers--16
Polyvinyl acetate--see Plastic adhesive
Poster paint--68
Power tools--138
Pre-bound books--81, 86
Press board--92
Press, book--see Book press
Pressure tape gilt--19
Pressurized cans--118
Private libraries--132-33
Pulp-wood stock--95
Puppies--37, 67-8

Rag paper--95
Readers, juvenile--82
Readers, stapled--81, 85
Re-bound books--10, 59, 60
Re-casing--67ff
Receiving desk--29, 30
Recipes--136
Records, hand-written--105, 136
Record-albums, phonograph--105ff
Red-tape--92
Reference stacks--89ff
Refrigerator jar (see also Jars)--13, 34, 114
Resin-based glue--130
Ring binders--103
Rondure--4, 69
Ruler--12, 15, 17, 61, 63, 70

Saddle soap--97ff
Saw, book-binder's--92
Saw, coping--92
School libraries--75ff
Scissors--12, 15, 17, 47, 76, 83, 104
Scores--see Music
Scrap books--136
Second-hand books--135ff

INDEX

Sets--66, 131
Sewing machine--21
Sheep-skin--see Leather
Sheet music--134
Sheeting--21
Shellac--see Book lacquer
Shoe polish, colorless--97, 100, 137
Side cover--1, 37, 38, 39, 41, 49, 51, 53, 54, 55, 57, 62, 63, 64, 65, 67, 70, 71, 72, 78, 79, 82, 83, 86, 95, 98, 99, 100, 109, 115, 134, 138
Signature--2, 3, 4, 40, 45ff, 49, 50, 52, 53, 138
Simulated leather--see Imitation leather
Sizing--98ff
Smock--39, 98
Soap--46, 109
Sorting--29ff
Spanish Royal library--59
Spare covers--68
Spine--1, 2, 30, 37, 38, 39, 41, 53, 59, 60, 61, 62, 63, 65, 67, 78, 79 (repair of), 83, 86, 95, 98, 100 (leather), 110, 112, 135, 137, 138
Sponge--97ff
Squirt-cans--118
Stacks
   damp--110
   reference--89ff
Stains, unidentified--116ff
Stapled readers--81, 85ff
Starch-based materials--114
Stitched hinge tape--21, 54ff, 82, 83, 85, 105
Stitching
   of hinge-tape--21, 53, 55, 56, 57, 83, 86
   of signatures--2, 46
Stock--3, 95, 107
Storage--see Supplies
Storage space--see Supplies
Street directories, paper-covered--111ff
Student-helpers--25-6, 75, 121ff
Stylus--18, 118
Suede brush--12, 14, 115
Super--3, 4, 21, 40, 50, 52, 53, 62

INDEX

Supplies
   ordering--26, 27
   storing--28
   testing new--26, 125
Suppliers--15, 28, 35
Supply closet--11, 22, 27
Surgical gauze bandage--21, 130, 138

Tape
   backing--84, 86-7, 112
   hinge--6, 7, 14, 21, 22, 30, 33, 35, 52, 54-6
   permanent mending--15, 17, 44, 76, 84, 106-7, 134
Technical books--115, 133
Technical libraries, private--133
Text books--131
Thread--45ff
Time--31, 93, 107
Tipping in--14, 45
Title--61, 89, 137
Title page--40, 67
Torn pages--15, 31, 44ff, 78, 84, 85
Town Hall records--133
Training menders--121ff
Transparent mending tape--see Permanent mending tape
Tree calf--99

Unbound magazines--see Periodicals

Vanilla--108
Vinegar--110
Viscosity--15, 34, 35, 77, 90, 115
Volunteers--26, 27

Warping--107ff
Washing
   books--31, 46ff, 109, 110
   menders--39
Waste-cloth, industrial--12, 13, 33, 36, 104
Water damage--107ff
Waterproofing--see Wax, waterproofing, Book lacquer
Waterproof ink--18, 118, 138

Wax, candle--see Wax, waterproofing
Wax, household--see Wax, waterproofing
Wax, waterproofing--7, 12, 14, 35, 62, 83, 88, 89, 91, 113, 116, 137, 138
Waxed paper--12, 14, 33, 36, 40, 44, 45, 51, 55, 56, 65, 71, 72, 76, 114
Weather
   effect on bookmobile collections--87
   effect on plastic adhesive--6, 34, 41, 51, 56, 79
   mildew--108, 110
Westerns--9
William Morris--62
Wire brush, suede--12, 14, 115
Wire clippers--103
Woven dress-maker's tape--21
Wrapping paper, brown--see Brown paper
Wrapper, plastic--36, 114
Wrinkles--34, 65, 108